THE in their own words

doors

contents

Perigee Books
are published by
The Putnam Publishing Group
200 Madison Avenue   New York, NY 10016

First Perigee edition 1991
Copyright © 1988 by Omnibus Press
(A Division of Book Sales Limited)
All rights reserved. This Book, or parts hereof,
may not be reproduced in any form without permission.

Library of Congress Cataloging-in-Publication Data
Doe, Andrew.
   The Doors in their own words / Andrew Doe and John
Tobler. — 1st Perigee ed.
     p.   cm.
   Reprint. Originally published: London : Omnibus Press,
© 1988.
   1. Doors (Musical group)   2. Rock musicians—
United States—Biography.   I. Tobler, John.   II. Doors
(Musical group)   III. Title.
ML421.D66D6 1991   90-7870 CIP MN
782.42166'092'2—dc20
[B]
ISBN 0-399-51659-X

Picture credits:
Joel Brodsky: Front Cover, p4.
Electra Records: p11, p12, p15, p38, p39, p56, p57, p64, p82.
LFI: p33, p44, p68, p69.
Barry Plummer: p16, p17, p49, p60, p83, p85, p92.
Pictorial Press: p8, p24, p25, p47, p54, p59, p77.
Rex Features: p2, p3, p18, p72, p78, p91, p96.
David Sygal: p14.
Chris Walter: p1, p5, p22, p70, p71, p74, p76, p84, p88, p93.

Printed in the United States of America
      4   5   6   7   8   9   10

This book is printed on acid-free paper.

intro

Nearly 20 years have passed since Jim Morrison, the charismatic vocalist with Los Angeles quartet The Doors, was reported to have died from a heart attack in Paris. There were some who doubted that Morrison was dead at all – he was embroiled in an oppressive court case resulting from an incident in Miami, where he allegedly exposed himself on stage, and many Doors watchers felt that he had simply gone to ground to allow the dust to settle, and would rise, as it were, from the dead when he considered that the time was right. We're still waiting, Jim . . .

Maybe it was because he was one of those who (apparently) died while at the height of their fame that Morrison and his surviving colleagues, Ray Manzarek (keyboards), Robbie Krieger (guitar) and John Densmore (drums), have enjoyed continuing celebrity

5

with generations not even born when he vanished.
A similar cult has arisen surrounding others, like
James Dean, Brian Jones, Jimi Hendrix, Buddy Holly
and many lesser names, where a career ended
prematurely. Past achievements gave promise of even
greater accomplishments which might have occurred
had a star survived, and whatever remained available
has continued to attract interest, be it records, films,
books or even likenesses.

The Doors were only active in their original form
for a period of about five years, and the number of
interviews given by Morrison was few, yet much of
what he did say has remained strangely relevant
to those who have only become aware of him in
retrospect. Which is not to say that Jim Morrison was
any kind of superhuman being; he was frequently
prone to excesses which were all too mortal.

While it must remain an irritation to his ex-colleagues,
whenever they are interviewed, Jim Morrison's name
is inevitably mentioned. Without their comments, plus
contemporary reviews and critiques from (mostly)
American magazines and newspapers, this book
would not have been a reality. The authors would like
to thank everyone whose words appear hereafter, and
hope that additional light has been shed on a subject
which has continued to fascinate – Jim Morrison.

early days & early Doors

1

Jim ''They claim everyone was born, but I don't recall it. Maybe I was having one of my blackouts.'' *(1969)*

John ''I grew up with Elvis Presley, Frankie Avalon, Fabian, all those guys. They were all making a social comment, their being was a social comment.'' *(1968)*

Ray ''My parents gave me piano lessons when I was around nine or 10, but I hated it for the first four, until I learned how to do it – then suddenly it became fun! I first heard race music, as it was then called, when I was about 12 or 13, and from that moment on I was hooked. I listened to the big disc jockeys in Chicago at the time – Al Benson, Big Al Hill – and my piano playing changed. I started to be influenced by jazz, learned how to play stride piano with my left hand, and I knew that was it – stuff with a beat. Blues, jazz, rock . . .'' *(1972)*

Jim ''The first time I discovered death . . . me and my mother and father, and my grandmother and grandfather, were driving through the desert at dawn. A truckload of Indians had either hit another car or something – there were Indians scattered all over the highway, bleeding to death. I was just a kid, so I had to stay in the car while my father and grandfather went to check it out. I didn't see nothing – all I saw was funny red paint and people lying around, but I knew something was happening, because I could dig the vibrations of the people around me, and all of a sudden I realised that they didn't know what was happening any more than I did. That was the first time I tasted fear . . . and I do think, at that moment, the souls of those dead Indians – maybe one or two of 'em – were just running around, freaking out, and just landed in my soul, and I was like a sponge, ready to sit there and absorb it . . .'' *(1970)*

Robbie ''There was a lot of classical music in my house – in fact, the first music I heard that I liked was 'Peter And The Wolf'. I think I was about seven. I listened to the radio a lot – Fats Domino, Elvis, The Platters. My father liked marching music, and I started playing trumpet when I was 10 but nothing came of that, so I began playing blues piano – without lessons – then at 17, I started playing guitar. Got my own when I was 18, a Mexican flamenco guitar, and I took flamenco lessons for a few months, until I saw Chuck Berry at the Santa Monica Civic. He was incredible. The next day, I went out and traded my classical in on a Gibson SG. I played that until it got ripped off, then got another. Records got me into the blues, too. The newer rock 'n' roll like Paul Butterfield. I wanted to learn jazz, really, but I got to know some people who did rock 'n' roll with jazz, and I thought I could make some money playing music.'' *(1978)*

Jim ''The most loving parents and relatives commit murder with smiles on their faces. They force us to destroy the person we really are: a subtle kind of murder . . .'' *(1969)*

John ''I got my first set of drums when I was in junior high: I played sort of symphonic music in high school – timpani, snare – then I played jazz for three years . . . sessions in Compton and Topanga Canyon. I was in a group called Terry Driscoll And The Twilighters, then Robbie and I were in a band called The Psychedelic Rangers, right before The Doors.'' *(1972)*

Robbie ''We recorded one song, 'Paranoia Blues'.'' *(1972)*

Jim ''I tried piano for a while, but I didn't have the discipline to keep it up. I think I got to about the third grade book.'' *(1969)*

Jim ''I was a good student – read a lot. But I was always talking when I wasn't supposed to, so they made me sit at a special table – nothing bad enough to get expelled for. I got through school. Went to Florida State University mainly because I couldn't think of anything else to do.'' *(1969)*

Robbie ''I would never have left school for any other group. I never thought I would leave school before getting my Master's degree.'' *(1967)*

Jim ''Ray and his brothers had a band, Rick And The Ravens . . .'' *(1969)*

Ray ''We played Friday and Saturday nights at The Turkey Joint West, two blocks from the beach at Santa Monica. I was still in school, so it was like a part-time job. I'd make about $35 a night, which was OK – it paid for the classes. That was the first time Jim ever sang on a stage: a whole bunch of guys from UCLA Film School would come down and there usually wasn't anyone in the place, so I'd call them all up on stage, and there'd be about 20 guys singing, jumping up and down, screaming songs like 'Louie Louie'.'' *(1972)*

Jim ''I never did any singing. I never even conceived it. I thought I was going to be a writer or a sociologist, maybe write plays. I never went to concerts – one or two at most. I saw a few things on TV, but I'd never been a part of it. I just got out of college and I went down to the beach.

I wasn't doing much of anything. I was free for the first time: I had been going to school constantly for 15 years. It was a beautiful hot summer, and I just started hearing songs. Those first five or six songs I wrote, I was just taking notes at a fantastic concert that was going on in my head . . . and once I'd written them, I had to sing them." *(1969)*

Ray "A beautiful California summer day, about the middle of August, and who should come walking down the beach but Jim Morrison. I said, 'Hey man, I thought you were going to New York.' He said, 'Well, I was, but I decided to stay here. I've been at a friend's house, up on his roof, writing songs.' I said, 'Aha! Why not sing one?' So what he did was to sing 'Moonlight Drive', and when I heard those first four lines, I said, 'Wow, those are the greatest lyrics I've ever heard for a rock 'n' roll song!' As he was singing, I could hear the chord changes and the beat – my fingers immediately started moving. I asked him if he had any more and he replied, 'Yeah, I've got a lot of 'em,' and he went through a few more, two or three others . . . and I said, 'Listen, those are the best rock 'n' roll songs I've ever heard – and I've been into music since I was seven years old. Why don't we do something about this?' Jim said, 'That's what I had in mind. Let's start a rock 'n' roll band together.' I said, 'Let's do that, and make a million dollars.' And that's how The Doors got started.

"Jim said 'We'll call it The Doors,' and I went, 'Whaaat? That's the most ridiculous . . . no, that's the *best* name I've ever heard for a rock 'n' roll band. The Doors . . . like the doors of perception,' and he said, 'That's it, the doors of perception, the Blake line.' If the doors of perception were cleansed, man could see things as they truly are; infinite. At the time, we had been ingesting a lot of psychedelic chemicals, so the doors of perception were cleansed in our own minds, and we saw the music as a vehicle to, in a sense, become proselytisers of a new religion, a religion of self, of each man as God. That was the original idea behind The Doors, using music and Jim's brilliant lyrics." *(1981)*

John "Their songs were really far-out to me. I didn't understand very much . . . but then I figured, I'm the drummer, not the lyricist." *(1972)*

Ray "At the time, I was involved with the Maharishi, who had just opened a meditation centre on 3rd Street, and in the initial class was John. I'd been talking to some guy about starting up a rock 'n' roll band, and he said, 'That guy over there is a drummer.' So I approached him, saying, 'Listen man, I'm a keyboard player and I have this great singer-songwriter, and we're trying to get a band together. We need a drummer – would you be interested?' He said, 'Sure, why not?' " *(1972)*

Jim "Rick And The Ravens had a contract with World-Pacific. They'd tried to get a couple of singles out, but nothing happened. They still had a contract to do a few sides, and we'd gotten together by then, so we went in and cut six sides in about three hours. At that time, Robbie wasn't in the band, but John was. He was drumming, Ray was on piano, I was singing and Ray's two brothers played harp and guitar . . . and there was a girl bass player – I can't remember her name." *(1969)*

John "Ray was singing harmonies on that record; his brother played piano." *(1978)*

Ray "It was funny – we walked the streets of Los Angeles with our demos, went to all the record companies and told them, 'Here are six songs. We have many more – listen to these.' And everyone, but everyone said, 'No, you can't – that's terrible – I hate it – no, no!' I especially recall a guy at Liberty: I played him 'A Little Game', saying 'You might like this one.' He listened, and then said, 'You can't do that kind of stuff!' Because it said things like 'go insane'. . .'' *(1972)*

Jim "I took the demos everywhere I could possibly think, just going in the door and telling the secretary what I wanted. Sometimes they'd say, 'Leave your number', sometimes they'd let you talk to someone else. The reception game. At Columbia, they became interested." *(1969)*

Ray "Billy James (of Columbia) said, 'I dig it', and recommended we be signed up." *(1972)*

Jim "We got a contract at Columbia for six months, during which time they were to produce

13

so many sides. Eventually, it turned out that no-one was interested in producing us, so we asked to get out." *(1969)*

Ray "A guy called Larry Marks came down to The London Fog one night, said, 'I'm your producer', and we never saw him again." *(1972)*

Ray "Billy James called up the Vox man and said, 'I'm sending these guys over, give them some equipment.' So we got a Vox organ – which was great – and a couple of amps, and that was about it." *(1980)*

Ray "Robbie came down with his guitar and bottleneck. When he put that big glass bottle on his finger and went 'boiiinnnngggg', I said, 'Whooaa, what a sound! Incredible! That's it, that's The Doors sound.' The first song we played as a group was 'Moonlight Drive', because it didn't have too many difficult chord changes, and after playing that, I said, 'This is it, this is the best musical experience I've ever had.' Of course, we were a little high at the time, but it was just . . . right, it was right from the beginning. The combination, the chemistry was right, the way John, Robbie and I, with our placid, meditation kind of thing, balanced off Jim's Dionysian tendencies. It was a natural – it couldn't miss. I thought, this is it, we're gonna make it. We're gonna make great music and the people are going to love it." *(1972)*

John "How we got into The London Fog was, we went down to the audition with about 50 of our friends to pack the place out – because it wasn't very big, about 15 by 40, and they all applauded us frantically. Jesse James, the owner, thought, 'My God!', and hired us. Next night, the place was kinda empty." *(1972)*

Ray "Nobody ever came in the place – the odd sailor or two on leave, a few drunks. All in all it was a very distressing experience, but it gave us time to get the music together. We had to play four or five sets a night. We'd start at nine and play 'til two with 15-20 minute breaks in between, and we had a chance to develop songs like 'Light My Fire', 'When The Music's Over' and 'The End'. 'The End' was originally a very short piece, but because of all the time we had to fill onstage, we took to extending songs, taking them into areas

we didn't know they would go into. Of course, we were playing stoned every night. It was the great summer of acid, and we really got into a lot of improvisation. I think the fact that nobody was at the club really helped us to develop into what The Doors became." *(1972)*

John "We dropped the other things in here and there because some of the audience were straights who'd be interested in dancing . . . so we'd play stuff like 'Louie Louie' just to get by, then we'd go back to our stuff." *(1978)*

Ray "We auditioned a few bass players, but either they didn't have the right personality or their chops weren't up to snuff, and after a while we thought, what are we going to do about a bass player? Maybe we won't use one at all . . . but I always felt we had to have somebody on the bottom, because I couldn't get it out of the Vox.

And it so happened that we auditioned for a gig at some club – which we failed, of course – and the house band there had this instrument called a Fender Rhodes piano bass, sitting on top of a Vox organ. When I saw it, I said, 'Eureka – I've found it! It sounds like a bass but you can play it like a keyboard . . .' I had always been trained in a boogie-woogie or stride piano technique, so my left hand always worked independently of my right anyway, so when I saw this bass, I knew I could play the bottom and leave my left hand free to improvise or whatever . . . so the hell with a bass player!" *(1972)*

John "I saw the drop list at Columbia – there were about 12 being picked up and 18 dropped . . . At the same time, we were really depressed, but later on, we realised it was great that we got out of that giant company thing, and we didn't get lost in the shuffle." *(1972)*

Ray "The owner of The London Fog eventually said, 'Listen you guys, you've been here for four months now, and I'm afraid we're going to have to get a new house band.' We thought, my God, what are we gonna do now? As the fates would have it, Ronnie Haran, the booking agent for the Whiskey A-Go-Go, came down to hear us, immediately fell in love with Jim, loved the music and asked, 'How would you guys like to be the house band at the Whiskey?' We said, 'Incredible – it just so happens we're free. Our engagement here is ended,' and we went from making $5 a night to union scale, $135 a week each – we felt like we were in heaven! We played with Them, Love, The Seeds, The Turtles, The Byrds. We were the openers." *(1972)*

John "The general idea was to blow the headliners off the stage." *(1972)*

Jim "The people said everyone in town was trying to sign us up, but it really wasn't true . . . in fact, Jac Holzman's might have been the only concrete offer we had. We may have made him come up with the best deal possible, but there's no question that we weren't that much in demand." *(1969)*

Robbie "I don't think it took him long to want to sign us, it just took a long time to work out the deal between the two parties . . . but I think Jac decided he wanted us the first time he saw us at The Whiskey." *(1980)*

John "As far as record people go, Jac Holzman was one of the better ones. We could really talk to him. He liked music . . . of course, we had our ups and downs with him, but he was one of the basic reasons we signed with Elektra. We thought, 'If they can make us as big as Love, that'll be fine'." *(1980)*

the albums

John "We always made an album as an album. We never really tried to make singles. We'd make the album, then when it was possible to be more objective about it, we'd sit back and maybe think, 'OK, what might be commercial for AM airplay?' We'd accept a little feedback from the record company on that, because having an AM single pushes the album, and you want to have people hear that." *(1978)*

Jim "To me, a song comes with the music, a sound or rhythm first; then I make up words as fast as I can, just to hold on the feel, until the music and lyric come almost simultaneously. With a poem there's usually no music. Most of my songs just came; I'm not a very prolific songwriter." *(1969)*

Robbie "We've always mixed our own albums. Mixing is half the album. Any band who doesn't do that isn't serious about their album." *(1980)*

Jim "I think albums have replaced books . . . and movies. A movie you might see once, maybe twice, then later on television. But an album, it's more influential than any art form going. Everybody digs them, and some you listen to about 50 times. You measure your progress mentally by your records." *(1969)*

John "Paul Rothschild was assigned to us by Elektra, and it was right for several albums. He was very eager to make it work, and so were we, so it was perfect." *(1977)*

Jim "A new album is like a new book." *(1968)*

'The Doors'
Robbie "Our album happened because we were in the right place at the right time." *(1972)*

Ray "The first album was an existential album. It's four incredibly hungry young men striving and dying to make it, desperately wanting to get a record, a good record, out to the American public and wanting the public to like the record. I feel any artist wants the public to like his act, or his record: I think that any artist creates from a driving inner need, but there's an outer need that's very important too, and that's acceptance by some people, somewhere, somehow. Someone saying to you, 'I like this work you've created.' That's what being an artist is. So 'The Doors' was that incredible, existential first time – 'Here they are, first time out, fresh, brand new and hungry as hell!'." *(1978)*

John "The whole first album was very quick – two weeks – because we had worked it up in the clubs, so we just went in and did it." *(1972)*

Ray "Our relationship with Paul was a marriage made in heaven. He was just what we needed. He came down to The Whiskey for a couple of nights, and we found him to be a man of like mind, someone who knew his poetry, knew his jazz, rock 'n' roll and folk, and was an excellent producer. He was very strong in the studio, yet knew enough to give us our heads when we needed to go in our own directions. He never really got in the way, never really said, 'Well, don't do it this way, do it that way.' Any suggestion he'd have to offer would be along the lines of, 'Listen you guys, what do you think about doing it this way?' Many times his suggestions were correct and so we'd say, 'OK, sounds like a great idea – let's do it that way.' Paul was an excellent manipulator in the studio." *(1972)*

Paul Williams/Crawdaddy " 'The Doors' is an album of magnitude. Thanks to the calm surefootedness of the group, the producer and the record company, there are no flaws; The Doors have been delivered to the public full-grown (by current standards) and are still growing (standards change). Gestation may have been long and painful; no-one cares. The birth of the group is in this album, and it's as good as anything in rock. The awesome fact about The Doors is that they will improve. This album is too good to be 'explained' note by note, song by song; that sort of thing could only be boring . . ." *(1967)*

Jim "Our first album, which a of lot people like, has a certain unity of mood, it has an intensity

about it, because it was the first album we'd recorded. And we did it in a couple of weeks; it came after a year of almost total performance, every night. We were really fresh and intense and together. Subsequent albums have been harder, but that's a natural thing. When we make a million dollars on each album, have a couple of hit singles from each, we can afford it. It's not always the best way, though." *(1969)*

Robbie " 'Light My Fire' . . . Ray had the idea for the opening part, which was the real hook; Jim helped me out on some of the lyrics, too, and the beat was John's idea." *(1972)*

Jim " 'The End' . . . I really don't know what I was trying to say. Every time I hear it . . . it means something else to me. It started off as just a simple goodbye song, probably to a girl, though I could see how it could be a goodbye to a kind of childhood." *(1969)*

Robbie "I'd heard John Hammond Jr. do 'Back Door Man', and that's where we got the idea from." *(1968)*

Ray "I had a record of Brecht/Weill songs, and 'Alabama Song' was just one of them, and we all liked it, and said, 'Let's give it a try'." *(1972)*

Robbie "Anybody's first album is always something special – an initial burst of energy. The trick is to keep that spontaneity." *(1967)*

John "We rehearsed for seven, eight months, then went around town playing anywhere that could take us for five months or so, so we really had a lot of material . . . had the first two albums wrapped up." *(1978)*

Pete Johnson/LA Times "The Doors, a quartet who have been playing in the Los Angeles area for some time, have come up with their first album . . . a strange new sound, but it is not strange in the fascinating directions pursued by The Rolling Stones, Dylan, Donovan or The Beatles.
"Jim Morrison, lead vocalist, has a voice similar to that of Eric Burdon . . . but he is somewhat overmannered, murky and dull. The best example of his faults is 'The End', an 11 minute 35 second exploration of how bored he can sound as he

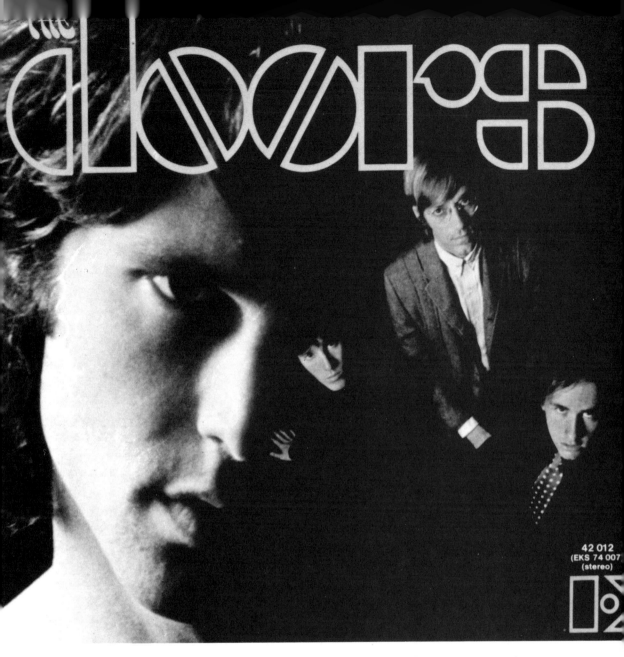

the doors

42 012
(EKS 74 007)
(stereo)

recites singularly simple, over-elaborate psychedelic *non sequiturs* and fallacies. Many of the numbers drag and there is an abundance of banal lyrics, but The Doors do sound fairly good on 'Break On Through', their current single, 'Twentieth Century Fox' and 'Alabama Song', which has good rhythm backing and passable harmony.'' *(1967)*

Ray ''We don't find our long numbers, they just come out. If a song needs six, eight, 10 minutes, it gets it.'' *(1969)*

Jim ''Once pieces like 'The End' and 'When The Music's Over' got on record, they became very ritualized and static. Those were constantly changing free-form pieces, but once we put them on record, they just kind of stopped, but they were at the height of their effect anyway, so it really didn't matter.'' *(1969)*

John ''The album is now totally different from where it was before. Someone wrote that our second album was totally different from the first one and that's true.'' *(1968)*

Ray ''The piano bass was OK for live work, but in the studio, it just didn't have any definition. It had a bad sound, didn't record well, so that's why I didn't use it after the first album.'' *(1972)*

21

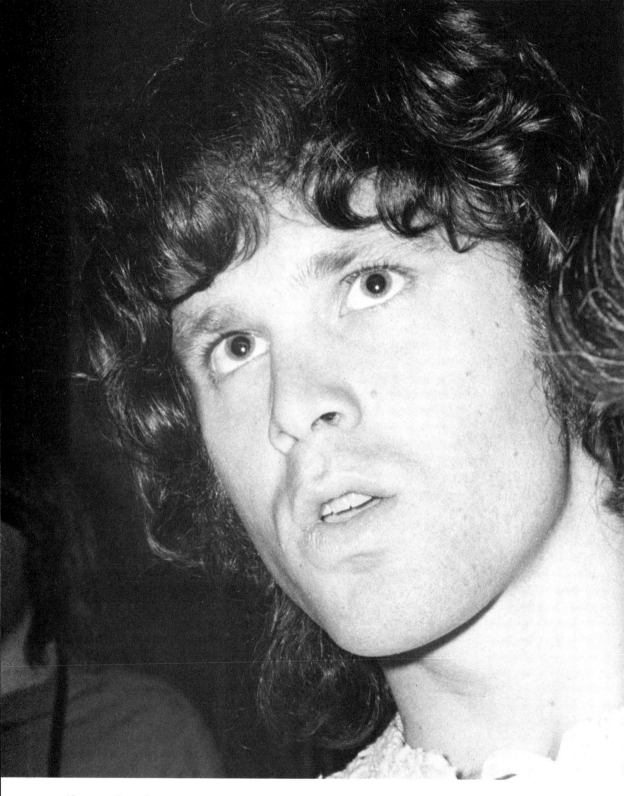

'Strange Days'

Richard Goldstein/Village Voice ''The Doors have had ample practice being themselves. They are one of the most oft-appearing groups in pop music, and this constant attention to live effect has produced a crackling confidence in each other's style which shows itself on their new album 'Strange Days'. The music is as tight and as controlled, as satisfying of its own aims as any I have heard in hard rock. Robbie Krieger's guitar slides and slithers around Jim Morrison's voice like a belly dancer. Ray Manzarek's rock organ continues to speak in an impressive array of languages (this album should enlarge the coterie of young musicians now applying a driving-yet-cool approach). Paul Rothschild's production is tastefully cut and tapered, and the album's jacket (let us offer thanks) is not art nouveau." *(1967)*

Jim "I hated the cover of our first album, so for 'Strange Days' I said, 'I don't want to be on this cover. Put a chick on it or something. Let's have a dandelion, or a design,' and because of the title, everyone agreed, 'cause that's where we were at, what was happening. It was right. Originally, I wanted us in a room surrounded by about 30 dogs, but we couldn't get the dogs. Everyone was saying, 'What are the dogs for?' And I said that it was symbolic that it spelled God backwards. Finally we ended up leaving it to the art director and the photographer. He came up with some freaks, a typical sideshow thing. It looked European." *(1968)*

Robbie "'Moonlight Drive' was the first song we recorded. Probably the reason it wasn't on the first album was, as it was the first one we did, it was probably the worst recorded, so we recut it for the second album: but I still have the tape, and it sounds pretty good." *(1972)*

Ray "'Strange Days' is when we began to experiment with the studio itself, as an instrument to be played. It was now eight-track, and we thought, 'My goodness, we can do this and that, now we've got eight tracks to play with.' It seems like nothing in these days of 32 or even 48-track recording, but to us, those eight tracks were really liberating. So, at that point, we began to play – it became five people: keyboards, drums, guitar, singer and studio." *(1978)*

Gene Youngblood/LA Free Press "The Doors new album 'Strange Days' is a landmark in rock music. It ventures beyond the conventional realms of musical expression: it has become theatre . . . The music of The Doors is more surreal than psychedelic, it is more anguish than acid. More than rock, it is ritual – the ritual of psycho-sexual exorcism. The Doors are the warlocks of pop culture. Morrison is an angel; an exterminating angel. He and The Doors are a

demonic and beautiful miracle that has risen like a shrieking phoenix from the burning bush of the new music." *(1967)*

Jim, (explaining 'Horse Latitudes') "It's about the Doldrums, where sailing ships from Spain would get stuck. In order to lighten the vessel, they had to throw things overboard. Their major cargo was working horses for the New World, and the song is about that moment when the horse is in the air. I imagine it must have been hard to get them over the side, 'cause when they got to the edge, they probably started chucking and kicking . . . and it must have been hell for the

men to watch, too, because horses can swim for quite a while, but then they lose their strength and just go down . . . slowly sink away." *(1967)*

Jim "When we became a concert group, recording group, when we were contracted to provide so many albums a year, so many singles every six months, that natural, spontaneous, generative process wasn't given a chance to happen, as it had in the beginning. We actually had to create songs in the studio . . . Robbie and I would just come in with a song and the arrangement already completed in our minds instead of working it out slowly." *(1969)*

'Waiting For The Sun'

Robbie "The 'third-album-syndrome': usually a group will have enough songs to record one, maybe two albums, then they'll go off on tour and not have the time to write any more material. So by the third album, you find yourself trying to write the stuff in the studio . . . and it shows, usually." *(1972)*

Pete Johnson/Philadelphia Enquirer

"The new album from The Doors is that difficult third LP which seems to thwart a number of contemporary pop groups. The Doors have succeeded. Their first two LPs were quite similar in both structure and in mood. Each contained an 11-minute fantasy number and some shorter songs whose fabric was trimmed from nightmarish visions and sexual images. Both were grotesque more than pretty. Both were also powerful enough to establish The Doors as the hottest group in the United States. 'Waiting For The Sun' contains the fewest snakes, the least ugliness, the lowest numbers of freaks and monsters, and the smallest amount of self-indulgent mysticism of the trio of Doors LPs. They have traded terror for beauty, and the success of the swap is a tribute to their talent and originality." *(1968)*

Jim "When we had to carry our own equipment everywhere, we had no time to be creative; now, we can focus our energies more intensively . . . the trouble is, we really don't see each other that much anymore. We're big time, so we go on tours, record and in our free time, everyone splits off into their own scenes. When we record, we have to get all our ideas then. We can't build them night after night like we used to in the clubs.

In the studio, creation isn't so natural." *(1969)*

John "By 'Waiting For The Sun', I was just frustrated. I was hinting that I was dissatisfied, wanting to drop out, whatever. The third album syndrome. Maybe I was trying to say to Jim, 'Don't be so self-destructive . . .'" *(1972)*

Bob Shayne/LA Free Press "This album is unbelievably bad, and it's embarrassing that it arrived on the same day as the first album by three groups – The Band, Notes From The Underground and Elizabeth – all vastly superior to the third album by the former next Beatles. 'Waiting For The Sun' contains three new versions of 'Break On Through', which go by the euphemisms 'Not To Touch The Earth', 'Unknown Soldier' and 'We Could Be So Good Together.' It contains 'Hello, I Love You', which was better when The Kinks did it as another song . . . It contains absolutely the worst lyrics I have ever heard in my life in 'Spanish Caravan'. The set has none of the vitality, originality, enigmatic quality, believable passion or musicality of the first two Doors LPs. Worst of all, I hear The Doors actually like this album. Perhaps they had better do something drastic to get their talents and tastes back into gear. I haven't given up on The Doors. I anxiously await their fourth album . . . but the spell isn't working this time." *(1968)*

'The Soft Parade'

John "We had a great time making that album . . . we spent more than $80,000 on it – we were making our 'Sgt. Pepper'. Just to show how ridiculous things got, we imported Jesse McReynolds and Jimmy Buchanan, a fiddler and a picker, from North Carolina, to play one solo on one song." *(1972)*

Ramblin' Jim/UCLA Daily Bruin "I find The Doors new LP an interesting paradox; I almost like it, but I still don't really like the group. Generally I enjoy their singles more than their other album cuts. This album is 5/9 single cuts from last year and somehow, despite the apparent economy of creativity, it strikes me as being a step forward for this band, which is often the target of critics expecting too many miracles. "The three hits are an interesting trio in themselves, 'Touch Me' being the shocking public

introduction to the orchestrated Doors. The LP's new cuts are quite a contrast. They are, for the most part, more predictably Door-ish, except for Ray's organ, which is used more as a rhythm instrument than the lead it used to be. Robbie Krieger's lead guitar is now more prominent, and he fits it into the group context well. "Basically, these are still The Doors that we have here. The orchestration is not too distracting, but, rather helpful. One of their old problems was that they exhausted the capacities of their instrumentation too quickly. Now, with other influences having their effect, the individuals are sounding better. Now, I can listen to The Doors without getting bored by the format." *(1969)*

John "I enjoyed it for what it was." *(1972)*

Robbie "'Touch Me' was originally 'Hit Me', but Jim said, 'No way am I going to sing those lyrics.' He thought they were too political . . . so we changed it." *(1970)*

Patricia Kennealy/Jazz & Pop (whose views, it must be noted, were highly coloured by her romantic involvement with Jim . . .) "'The Soft Parade': none of it is bad, most of it is very superior music and some of it is absolutely glorious. The first major bitch – of two – is that, of the nine songs presented, five were released in single versions over the past eight months. The other complaint is the orchestration. Paul Harris' arrangements are, for the most part, tasteful and effective, and The Doors are smart enough to use the backing, not just let it happen

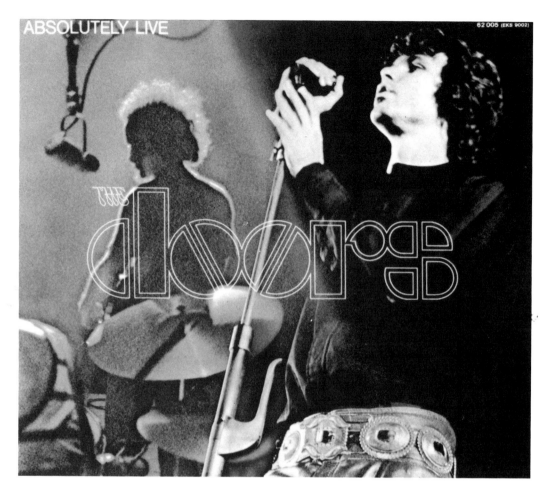

ABSOLUTELY LIVE

62 005 (EKS 9002)

or, worse, use them. The biggest loser, though, is Ray Manzarek. Ray, who plays an ascetic, thoughtful, professorial and appealing organ, is very often snowed under by the brass Harris has added, and most of the time he is dastardly under-recorded." *(1969)*

Robbie "We liked it, but no-one else seemed to." *(1972)*

Jim "It kinda got out of control, and took too long in the making. It spread over nine months. An album should be like a book of stories strung together, some kind of unified feeling and style about it, and that's what 'The Soft Parade' lacks." *(1970)*

'Morrison Hotel'

Robbie "We listened to 'The Soft Parade' a couple of times, and decided it would probably sound just as good without the brass." *(1972)*

Bruce Harris/Jazz & Pop "The Doors fifth

album is not what it seems. And anyone who tells you it's The Doors return to that 'good old rock 'n' roll' has either confused Fabian with Walt Whitman, or has just been listening to The Moody Blues for far too long. No, The Doors have revived, even resurrected, a lot of lost arts in 'Morrison Hotel', which lyrically encompasses everything from poetry to parable, but in their hands, rock 'n' roll and all its magic have always been full of life and have never needed any special care. All Doors albums have been deeply autobiographical, especially the unjustly criticized 'Soft Parade' which was really a whole lot better than an awful lot of awful people wanted to have to admit. 'Morrison Hotel', for all its flurries of autobiography, is really more directly an album about America . . . and there can be little doubt that 'Morrison Hotel' is one of the major musical events of Rock '70." *(1970)*

Jim "Our music has returned to the earlier form, using just four instruments. We felt we'd gone too far in the other direction, ie, orchestration and wanted to get back to the original basic format." *(1970)*

'Absolutely Live'
Jim "I think it's a true document of one of our good concerts: not insanely good, but a true portrait of what we usually do on a good night." *(1970)*

Don Heckman/New York Times "Double-disc chronicles of live concerts seem to be the thing these days, and understandably so, I guess, since already recorded material can be sold once again, this time with the added energy of an enthusiastic audience. But there's the danger, too, that less-than-super talent will have trouble surviving such repeated exposure. I think it's going to sound like sacrilege to suggest that the Doors have over-extended themselves with this collection, but that's precisely what has happened. Musically, the group has never been much to brag about, dependent as they are on seemingly endless explorations of single-chord tunes. As a style, it was OK for the early days of tripping West Coast rock, but in today's market, it's beginning to sound as dated as a Frankie Avalon surfing song." *(1970)*

John "Getting the live album to work, and doing it, took a lot longer than we'd thought, so it came out a lot later than we'd all wanted. We wanted to do it a lot earlier." *(1977)*

R Meltzer/Twenty Minute Fandangoes
"'Absolutely Live' is a great party album. And what makes parties what they are? Food mostly, since fun and companionship can be had even away from parties and music can be had from the radio or TV. So, with the right food to accompany it, this can be the most memorable disc of the second half-century." *(1970)*

'13'
Ray "We never wanted them to do that. We had nothing to do with that album at all." *(1972)*

Dave Marsh/Creem "The saving grace of this album is that those FM DJs are now so bored that they'll play anything new. Anyway, there are at least 13 classic songs . . . Even if the mere existence of this album is a tad like the male nipple (totally unfunctional except in terms of arousal and desire for more) and even totally consumeristic, you might want to pick it up." *(1970)*

'LA Woman'

Robbie " 'LA Woman' was our biggest album since 'The Doors', I think. Jim loved LA: 'LA Woman' is a kind of compliment song." *(1978)*

Ray "It was back to basics, back to the roots. W brought microphones and recording equipment right into the rehearsal room. Instead of using a professional studio, we said, 'Hey, let's record this album where we rehearse and let's have a spontaneous, live kinda feel.' We brought Jerry Scheff in on bass and Marc Benno on rhythm guitar – we'd never used a rhythm guitar player before – so we had six musicians all going at the same time. 'LA Woman' is a live take – Jim sang the song while we played it. There were very few overdubs, an absolute minimum. I think I overdubbed a tack piano on 'LA Woman' . . . and that's about it. Everything else was an actual live recording, as if it were done on stage. That's why it sounds so fresh." *(1972)*

Robbie "It was a mutual thing, really. We found out that after four or five albums, a group learns how to get what they want in the studio, and Paul didn't really have anything more to say that we didn't already think of ourselves, so he wasn't really a necessary factor any more. He didn't feel he was contributing enough to be the producer. He's one of those producers who really has to get his whole trip into the thing, put his whole energy into it, into what he's doing . . . and this time, we knew what *we* wanted." *(1972)*

R Meltzer/Rolling Stone "Besides being heavy in their early days, The Doors were funny too. Funnier than a fish, Morrison was an earnest drinker, which of course helped. Now he's drinking more than ever, hence there's some material basis for all the laughs. And since heaviness has been kicked in the ass of late, all the kickers owe it to themselves to sit down with this one. There isn't one serious cut on the entire album. Jim's taking no chances about being taken seriously, or with universal import. In fact, he's not even writing his own snake lyrics anymore. Instead, there's John Lee Hooker's 'Crawling King Snake', a whopper of a ready-made and proof positive that he and his boys are still listening to the roots . . . On it, Morrison demonstrates his final grasp of all the vocal chicanery only hinted at

in flashes on 'Love Street'. And he's even a fair-to-middlin' blues gomper because, for the first time, he honestly doesn't give a donut about how authentic any of that whole thing sounds. He was never actually Eric Burdon, but his trans-racial bravado at least hinted at some intent in that direction. Now all the cards are on the table . . . And what's more, Jim's back-up band has finally reduced its approach to one of ping-ponging the essential free-as-air spirit the man's been toying with ever since he abandoned Howlin' Wolf for Mel Tormé.

"In other words, The Doors have never been more together, more like The Beach Boys, more like Love. In terms of what they're after here, The Doors as a band never falter and there isn't one bummer cut on the entire album – obviously a first for them. You can kick me in the ass for saying this (I don't mind): this is The Doors greatest album (including their first) and the best album so far this year. A landmark worthy of dancing in the streets." *(1971)*

John " 'LA Woman' was so much fun to do . . . I don't think we do long numbers just to make them long. They just come out to what they are. Maybe recording in our own little studio loosened us up, and we felt like playing longer." *(1972)*

Rob Houghton/Creem "Warm blooded animals seem to loathe reptilian forms of life. That might have been the reason for the incredible wellsprings of disgust that washed over The Doors, who were almost universally loved, after Jim Morrison proclaimed himself to be The Lizard King. No other rock group went so dramatically from a position of admiration to sheer hatred in such a short time as did The Doors. Something about them must have just rubbed people the wrong way. It couldn't have been the music. The Doors are infinitely greater musicians than groups like, say, The Grateful Dead. The Summer Of Love was a long time ago, and those first experimental, 'trippy', acid-rock albums sound so quaint and transparent that they would be funny if they weren't so embarrassing.

"By contrast, The Doors first album has lost none of its hard onyx sheen that will make it a rock 'n' roll classic . . . 'LA Woman' is the last album of the present Doors contract with Elektra. Too much

passes away from us too quickly these days. Are we really going to be better off if Jim Morrison becomes a singles act? What I'm trying to say is that we should hold on to those things that have value . . . Let's make sure that 'LA Woman' will not be the album that will finally close The Doors.'' *(1971)*

Jim ''At last, I'm doing a blues album.'' *(1970)*

'Other Voices'

Ray ''At first, we were very unsure of ourselves – we didn't know exactly what we were going to sound like. We knew that the music would be OK, but we weren't too sure about the vocals, how they were gonna sound. We didn't know how it was going to gel . . . but little by little, it all began falling together.'' *(1972)*

Ben Gerson/Rolling Stone ''Drums, keyboard, guitars require a certain minimal technique but singing – well, anyone in rock 'n' roll can be a singer. With this assumption, Krieger, Manzarek and Densmore have gallantly persevered. There is no structural reason why The Doors should not continue, and so they do. Yet while it would be unfair to say The Doors were simply the embodiment of Jim Morrison, it is obvious that Morrison was more than just a singer. Now, sadly, he's gone for good, and his three colleagues are making a try at standing on their own.

''There is no question that there was more to The Doors' identity than Morrison, for the material here is still basically Doors. Yet it is Doors music mainly in its trappings. Because the risks run are fewer, it can be less bad than their previous output, but it is, overall, most certainly less good. The material is weak, the singing colourless, the playing irrelevantly consistent. They are still The Doors, but they are Doors without a cause or a passion, however awkward and uncommunicative those passions could sometimes be. Which, I wonder, is the more acceptable – to say that The Doors are better without Morrison, or that they were better with him? Matching or surpassing what they did with him might seem almost disrespectful, which could make it mighty tough for the new Doors to make a go of it.'' *(1971)*

Ray ''Yes, we thought about finding another singer, but it seemed kinda impossible to bring in another personality . . . and what if he wasn't the right guy? And, of course, it would be really hard on him too, because he'd always be Jim's replacement.'' *(1978)*

John ''A couple of the songs have been around for a year or so, but the rest are new . . . they might be songs we'd thought of doing, but it wasn't right then.'' *(1971)*

Steve Gettinger/Salem Capitol Journal

"Perhaps the second-greatest tragedy (after the personal one) about the premature death of Jim Morrison, was that it came just as The Doors seemed to be making a comeback. If he had died before 'LA Woman' came out, not nearly so many people would have cared. Now the remaining Doors are trying to make it as a trio: the notes for the album make but a passing reference to Morrison. Perhaps the break is too clean. Morrison would have certainly kept his boys from doing anything so trite as 'Down On The Farm'. And his talents as a lyricist are sorely missed. It would appear that it was his lyrics which provided the impetus for the other's intense psychological instrumentation, for the whole album here seems to lack guts.

"The emphasis here is on a softer sound, but only occasionally does it come off as anything more than derivative. 'Ships w/Sails' has a passably pretty melody, and a couple of the other tunes have at least a mild swing to them. But overall, it seems safe to say that The Doors are dead. If Manzarek, Densmore and Krieger were three chaps who wandered in off the street, this material would never have been recorded. Be grateful for what we got, years ago." *(1971)*

Ray "I think it's going to take people a little while to adjust to what we're doing. At first, I think it might be rather confusing for them, but if they'll just listen, and dig the music . . ." *(1971)*

'Full Circle'

Buck Sanders/Creem "An optimistic Doors album? Fact is, every single one of The Doors albums was optimistic: make me smile, anyway. What 'Full Circle' is, is distinctly unimportant. When you pass through the midsection of the infinity loop, full circle in other words, what happens is that you squeeze out the intellectual doo-doo, and that's what The Doors have done for this album. I've had trouble getting past side one. In fact, I don't care about getting past side one . . . if I say it's perfect music for a coke date at the local teen club, you might get me wrong . . ." *(1972)*

John "In retrospect, 'Full Circle' was a bit of a disaster, but at the time, we had our hearts in it. Then, about halfway through, the songwriting thing started to get on everyone's nerves. Which song are we going to do? Ray's turning this way, Robbie's going that way, so it all got a little bit touchy, which is why I don't think our album turned out all that well." *(1977)*

'An American Prayer'

John "I just happened to be thinking about the poetry Jim recorded about five years back – I guess someone must've mentioned it to me or something – so I called up John Haney, who engineered the sessions and asked, 'What happened to Jim's poetry tapes? Do you have any copies?' The guy said, 'Better than that, I have the originals. Why don't you and the other guys come over? We can listen to them, see if there's anything there, and maybe we could do something with them.' And that's how it all got started." *(1978)*

Robbie "There was no way to tell how long something was going to take. It turned out that for just about everything we said, 'OK, this shouldn't take more than a month', it took about three." *(1978)*

Ray " 'An American Prayer' was a private edition that Jim handed out to friends and certain fans, and over the years, I've had many people come up to me and ask, 'How do I get a copy of it? I've heard about it and want to read it.' So naturally, we thought it would have to be included on the album. It was so good, we felt it belonged in a larger scope than just 500 copies out there somewhere." *(1978)*

Dick Nusser/Billboard "It would be misleading to label this album merely a collection of the late Jim Morrison's poetry set to music, for much of the best of rock 'n' roll is poetry set to music. Granted, the words were recorded alone by Morrison and the music, by the original Doors, was added recently. But, who is to say that, had he lived, The Doors wouldn't have recorded an album much like this at some date?

" 'An American Prayer', on its own merits, ranks among The Doors' finest works, on a par with the albums that made them overnight sensations following the release of 'Light My Fire'. Words aside, it is loaded with melody and the infectious yet simple musical hooks The Doors always applied to Morrison's lyrics. The opening cut pulsates with a rhythm track that smacks of today's disco best, but it primarily serves to punctuate the lyric. Following 'Awake' the music and words continue to compliment each other. The music is ominous: the words are brutal, frank and honed to a fine point. 'The Poet's Dream', a collection of facile, following lines from Morrison's stream of consciousness – or unconsciousness, as the case may be – is as complete a synthesis of late 1960s consciousness as anything that has been written, filmed, sung or played since that decade ended.

"There are complete songs on this record. While some may be familiar to Doors fans, others are not. They speak for the moment and have obviously been chosen with care, thought, and are by no means fillers, but rather as interludes to remind us of The Doors' musical power, and the fact that what we're hearing is still rock 'n' roll." *(1978)*

Ray "It was a difficult album to put together because there was so much material to choose from, to put into perspective. We tried to make it, in a sense, biographical. The first part is his childhood, the second part high school, the third part the young poet, stoned on a rooftop in Venice with acid dreams. The Doors are the fourth part, and the fifth is a final summation, in a way, of the man's entire life and his philosophy." *(1978)*

John "This is Jim's poetry album – he never got to finish it, so now Ray, Robbie and I are doing it for him. It's going to be like a biography. It's Jim's life, really." *(1977)*

Ray "Jim's poetry wasn't necessarily written poetry. I always considered him to be back in the classic Greek tradition of a spoken poet, a man who gets up on stage and recites his poetry to handclaps or a drumbeat, or an implied beat. Jim always had this implied sense of rhythm in his poems, so therefore it was pretty easy for us, as musicians, to look into a rhythm one way or another. When we heard the poems, we thought, 'OK, here's this implied rhythm – let's just make it explicit.' 'Ghost Song', for example, in the end, Jim gets to talking about dead Indians on the highway, so we knew that required an Indian beat. So, John got off on the drums with this tom-tom beat, and from that I put an Em7/Em9 on top, feeling the same rhythm. Robbie started on his guitar, a couple of little licks and lines, and then on top of that, we just put Jim's poetry, we spaced it out a little bit, made a few cuts here and

there, kinda, 'Wait Jim, wait four bars and let us play this little line, and then you can come back again.' It was almost like working with the man in person. It was a very eerie feeling, because Jim was really there at rehearsals. It was the three of us and Jim on tape. OK, so he wasn't there in person, but his presence was almost tangible. Recording the new stuff took about two months.'' *(1978)*

John ''Jim's getting back at us. This time, it's like he's saying, 'OK, now it's your turn to

do the overdubs!'" *(1978)*

Terry Rompers/Trouser Press Collectors Magazine "Assembled with the co-operation and musical contributions from the three Doors who survived Morrison, this audio document

blends all the singer's aspects – songwriter, poet, storyteller, bullshitter, degenerate scatologist – into an album that amounts to an annotated Doors guide book, loosely presenting different stages of development in a way that exposes little and suggests much. Morrison's contributions are spoken passages taped with no intention of release: reasonably apt music was added long afterwards. There is something queer about this, but because of the people involved, there is none of the detachment that plagues those posthumous Jimi Hendrix releases.

"'An American Prayer' is a lot more than slapdash songs created from poems and subsequent music. The informed juxtaposition draws arrows and leads to conclusions. The fine line between poetry and life is erased; confusion instilled by tape cutters makes it impossible to gauge what Morrison actually created, and what has been spliced into reality. Social mores of the late seventies permit the release of sexually explicit material that would never have been considered when Morrison was alive, though nothing is too shocking here. This album shows what Morrison was, not what The Doors were. It's a unique piece of work, and in no way exploits or abuses those unable to defend themselves.

The best moments enrich Doors songs with poetry: a bit of 'The WASP' overdubbed with Morrison reciting the lyrics; a doped-out story that leads into 'Peace Frog'. A strong, live 'Roadhouse Blues' is another highlight, although it finishes with a horribly dated rap to the audience. 'Lament For My Cock' shows just how obsessive Morrison was about sex, but avoids mere vulgarity. This is Morrison at his most transparent and alone. This record defies categorization, but should hold great significance for anyone who was ever moved by Jim Morrison – man or legend." *(1980)*

Ray "I hope the people who are going to listen to this album will perceive that it's quite a unique experience . . . it's not something to put on while you're doing the dishes, or mending the car. You have to put this record on, sit down and listen. It demands. All it asks for is 40 minutes of your time, and if you'll give those 40 minutes, we'll take you somewhere that maybe you've never been before." *(1978)*

the
concerts

Jim "There's nothing more fun than to play music to an audience. There's this beautiful tension. There's freedom, and at the same time, an obligation to play well. I love it, the way an athlete loves to run, to keep in shape. Some of the best musical trips we ever took were in clubs. There's much less bullshit. If it doesn't cut it, everyone knows." *(1969)*

John "Our concerts are totally different from our records. I mean, it's theatre. You have to see us perform in person – we're totally different from the way we are on our records." *(1968)*

Robbie "It was kinda fun, but we were in such big halls that it was hard to get the sound right. I really liked it more when we were on the way up – at clubs like the Whiskey, and in New York. Once we started the concerts, it was more showtime, and I didn't like that as much." *(1970)*

Jim "A game is a closed field, a ring of death with sex at the centre, and performing is the only game I've got." *(1969)*

Ray "When you saw us in 1967, you knew nothing about us, and all of a sudden, you were being tripped out." *(1972)*

Francine Grace/Los Angeles Times "The group, four long-haired Venice boys in their early twenties, were at UCLA when they banded together just over a year ago. The Doors weld a rock 'n' roll beat with continuous jazz improvisation to produce an intense, highly emotional sound. They call their music 'primitive and personal' and find it hard to work without audience reaction. Their numbers change constantly at live shows, and new ones are written as they perform. 'We just play and it kinda happens,' said one of the group. Numbers start up with the unhurried loud wail of an electric organ, joined by a low groaning electric guitar and backed up by a steady drum. The words build with the music into an accelerating crescendo of frenzied sound. Trying to avoid the 'hard, straight sound' of many rock groups, The Doors aim for dramatic impact in their music. Gazzari's crowded dance floor proves that The Doors lyrical freedom hasn't hurt their strong rock 'n' roll tempo." *(1967)*

John "It was total theatre. It wasn't planned or conceived in the studio, it was fairly subconscious. Jim was magical – he never knew quite what he was going to do each night, and that's what was so exciting, the suspense, because obviously we didn't really know either. Our music was the framework, but it didn't seem that rigid: somehow we could go off at a tangent for 20 minutes or so, and Jim would stretch out, improvise some poetry, and we'd vamp along, comment on his poetry, improvise a while, then we'd get back into the chorus of the song . . . that was what made it so exciting. Plus, he had a great rapport with the audience. He could really work 'em up!" *(1978)*

Jim "A Doors concert is a public meeting called by us for a special kind of dramatic discussion and entertainment. When we perform, we're participating in the creation of a world, and we celebrate that with the crowd. It becomes the sculpture of bodies in action. That's politics, but our power is sexual . . . maybe you could call us erotic politicians. We're a rock 'n' roll band, a blues band, just a band, but that's not all – we make concerts sexual politics. The sex starts with me, then moves out into the charmed circle of musicians on stage, then the music we make goes out to include the audience and interacts with them: they go home and interact with the rest of reality, then I get it all back by interacting with that reality . . . so the whole sex thing works out to be one big ball of fire." *(1969)*

Robbie "He used to listen, stop and listen to what the audience had to say. We didn't know what the hell was going on." *(1972)*

Pete Johnson/Los Angeles Times "The Doors are a hungry-looking quartet with an interesting original sound, but what is possibly the worst stage appearance of any rock 'n' roll group in captivity. The lead singer emotes with his eyes closed, the electric pianist hunches down over his instrument as if reading mysteries from the keyboard, the guitarist drifts about the stage randomly, and the drummer seems lost in a separate world . . ." *(1967)*

Jim "The only time I really open up is on stage. I feel spiritual up there. Performing gives me a mask, a place to hide myself where I can reveal myself. I see it as more than performing, going on, doing songs, and leaving. I take everything personally, and don't really feel I've done a complete job unless we've gotten everybody in the theatre on common ground." *(1969)*

Paul Williams/Crawdaddy "The Doors, in person, have become the best the West has to offer. In concert at the Village Theatre several weeks ago, they were frightening and beautiful beyond my ability to describe. Robbie, John and Ray excelled in musicianship, constantly adding to the perfection of their album (now number two in the country) and leaving no note unturned in their desire to communicate. And, as it was meant to be, Jim Morrison stole the show. Jim brilliantly carried the audience from anticipation to excitement to over-the-edge fright and joy . . . and the second show made the first an introduction. The Doors are now the best performers in the country, and if albums are poetry as well as music, then the stage show is most of all drama, brilliant theatre in any sense of the word. Artistic expression transcending all form, because you knew that as Jim died for you there on stage, that it was not mere acting, but it

was all for art. And Jim dies a little more each day, frightening and beautiful as he strains to perfect his art." *(1968)*

Ray "Time would be suspended. Time would actually stop. The only thing that would exist would be the energy, the feeling generated between the audience and the band. The one common thing was the rhythm, the power of the beat: it became an hypnotic drone that captured the conscious mind and lulled it into a non-state, allowed you to sink down a little lower into your subconscious mind. That's what happened at a Doors concert. Jim was in control of these people, and they allowed him to take them on a psychic journey – to suspend reality and the Universe, and to examine the depths of the human psyche." *(1980)*

Jim "I just try to give the kids a good time." *(1969)*

Jim "It's a search, an opening of one door after another. Our work, our performing, is a striving for a metamorphosis. Right now, we're more interested in the dark side of life, the evil thing, the night time. But through our music, we're striving, trying to break through to a cleaner, freer realm. Our music and personalities as seen in the performance are still in a state of chaos and disorder, with maybe an element of purity just showing. Lately, when we've appeared in concert, it's started to merge . . ." *(1968)*

Fred Powledge/Wicked Go The Doors "Troy isn't exactly the boondocks, but it appeared that night to be in a state of morbidity. The concert there was a bomb. Morrison arrived late and moody, and swaggered on to the stage in front of six huge amplifier-speakers that pushed 1350 watts of audio power, and he did his best . . . but the crowd wasn't ready for music that celebrated the black evil side. The music was plenty wicked, but the crowd seemed to be treating it as entertainment rather than an invitation to wallow. To them, Morrison wasn't dangerous; he was just a poet. He sang for 45 minutes and, when he came off stage, said to his colleagues, 'Let's see how they liked us.' There was no encore. The applause quickly died down, people started to leave, and The Doors hurriedly returned to the airport . . .

"The New Haven audience was much sharper than the college students of Troy had been, and Morrison felt the difference. The crowd applauded at the right times – there were maybe 2000 people there, and most of them were getting bammed on the music and words. Morrison bummed a cigarette from the audience, and a little later, threw a microphone stand offstage. On one occasion, he spat towards the front row, but he fell short, and nobody seemed to care.

"He was dangerous, but danger was part of the show. His performance had the same elements of carnality as it had in Troy the night before, but here the audience was getting with it too, they were part of the music. Manzarek continued on the electric organ, Krieger on the guitar, Densmore on the drums; and Morrison started talking.

" 'I want to tell you about something that happened just two minutes ago right here in New Haven . . . this is New Haven, Connecticut, United States of America?' The crowd grew quieter. Morrison started talking about having eaten dinner, and about having a few drinks and about somebody having asked for his autograph at the restaurant, and about having talked with the waitress about religion, and about coming over to the New Haven arena for the concert, and about going into the dressing room and meeting a girl there, and talking with her. 'We started talking,' he said, still keeping the rhythm that Densmore was beating behind him, twisting the microphone, making you understand that he was on the black, evil side. 'And we wanted some privacy, so we went into the shower-room, we were not doing anything you know, just standing there and talking. And this little man came up, this little man, in a little blue suit and a little blue cap, and said, 'Watcha doin' there?' 'Nothin',' but he did not go away, he stood there and then he reached around behind him, and he brought out this little can of somethin', looked like shaving cream, and then he sprayed it into my eyes. I was blinded for about 30 minutes!!!'

"The lights came on, Morrison blinked out into the audience. He asked why they were on. There was no reply. Manzarek walked over and whispered something into his ear. Morrison asked if the crowd wanted more music. The crowd screamed, 'Yes!' 'Well, turn off the lights. TURN OFF THE LIGHTS!' A policeman walked on to the stage, arresting the singer. Morrison was nonchalant at first: he even pointed his mike at the policeman and said, 'Say your thing, man.' But another cop snatched the mike from Morrison's hand.

"People scrambled off the stage. Bill Siddons, The Doors' road manager, tried to protect Morrison's body from the cops with his own. They then took Morrison away, and Siddons tried to protect the equipment, and he thrashed around on the stage as more policemen ran in. Some of the crowd started to leave, some stayed around and, in protest, pushed over the folding wooden chairs . . ." *(1968)*

Jim "We have fun, the cops have fun, the kids have fun. It's a kind of weird triangle." *(1969)*

Jim "London was the best, I'd say. They really liked it. The rest was neither here nor there: limited enthusiasm. I got the idea that they didn't like or dislike it . . . they didn't know how to express what they felt about it. But they really take music seriously over in Europe. It's not just the province of kids – they discuss it." *(1968)*

Robbie "The European audience didn't really know the whole Jim Morrison superstar trip – it was just The Doors. They didn't really know who the lead singer was, and they loved it." *(1969)*

Robbie "With The Beatles and The Stones, it was the girls going crazy . . . but with The Doors, there were actually young guys going nuts with high energy releases, and destroying stuff . . ." *(1980)*

Ray "I'd rather play for 20 million acid-heads than a convention of beer-drinkers." *(1971)*

Tim Boxell/Minneapolis Daily "I was looking forward eagerly to The Doors concert. Even as influenced as it was by too much Hamm's beer, it was something else. People who came to hear cuts from their albums flawlessly duplicated must have been disappointed, for Morrison seemed quite bored by all the old Doors material, which with the beer and the standard performer's response to playing Minneapolis, added up to ineffectively delivered numbers laden with ad-libs and vulgarities. The appearance of a local blues harpist, and a change to blues material, brought Morrison around. Ray Manzarek seemed to respond as well. Backed by Densmore's beat, Morrison managed to do some of the singing that he has become known for. The standard closing 'Light My Fire' was a return to lethargy, in spite of a dynamic effort by the rest of the group.

"The concert was only a success by grace of Morrison's initial effect as a superstar, and a very good poet, and by the hard work of the rest of the band. Morrison broke off in nearly every song after the first couple of stanzas, leaving it up to the others to improvise until he was ready to sing again. This may be one reason why the rest of the group is so good. Watching Morrison himself was a great part of the show, and he could hold your attention sitting down, but in the rows further back, people were more dependent on their ears than their eyes, and it really must have dragged at times.

"Yet a concert by The Doors is supposed to be something out of the ordinary. People come to see The Doors as much for their music as for their unpredictability. The Doors come to affect you and create a response, and the one they created depended on you, and on what they want to do. Morrison instrumented the effect this time. He didn't give the audience what they expected. He gave them what they wanted, he gave them The Doors." *(1969)*

51

John "The kids get bammed with the music and the lights and the words, and they just go, 'Uhhhhnn,' and they dig it. They don't worry about anything." *(1968)*

Ray "People were just coming to see Jim Morrison, that guy in leather, the Acid King, the Lizard King. Let's go see a geek, the guy's stoned all the time and he puts on a helluva show . . . Well, he did put on a helluva show, but it wasn't because he was stoned. It was a psychological/ horror/freak show, a freak show in the shamanistic sense – the sense of possession, the sense of participating with the powers of the universe that Jim was capable of doing. The people who came to the early Doors shows came to see that." *(1980)*

Jim "I wonder why people like to believe I'm high all the time? Maybe they think someone else can take their trip for them . . ." *(1969)*

John Carpenter/Los Angeles Free Press
"The Doors. Well, there is a good group in that mish-mash of reptilian, college-kid, rebellious hype. Manzarek and Krieger are not without their

merits as musicians. The group's recorded sound is more interesting, more creative than 90 per cent of the groups around today. But that's music. That is not why they are a 14,000 draw. Jim Morrison brings the people. Jim is who the spectators want to see get outrageous, just like they read he did in Phoenix and San Jose. Riots, action – the group is banned in a half-dozen cities, so much is expected.

"From the restlessness that ran through the crowd until The Doors came on stage, pop music was not what the people came for. That is fine.

Why should they expect less than they've been told is there? As it turned out, they didn't get it and went home dragged, and feeling burned and cheated, bugged because they were cheated of their extra big moment – the moment when Morrison, they had read, would do something outrageous. After each song, the stage darkened and the audience yelled out fave Doors songs to the lit cigarettes floating about on the stage. Morrison, ever the pro, tested the gathering, tossing cigs into the crowd. No riot, The 'Stick The Maracas Down Into The Crotch And Then Throw

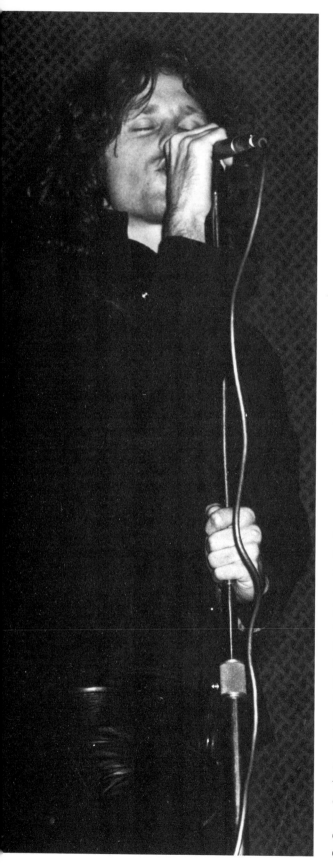

Them To The Fans' number. No riot. Finally, another posture at the brink as Morrison to the multitude speaks, crouched in a squat at the foot of a ramp protruding from the stage. He says, 'We can play music all night if that's what you want, (Cheers) but that's not what you want. You don't really want that, do you? (He giggles). You want something more, something different, something you ain't never seen before, don'tcha?'

"Indeed, that is what the poor creeps came in for, and rightly so too. That is what The Doors publicity mill has been building all these months. It was 14,000 roller-derby pop fans waiting for the crack-up, the Naked Door, that one time when the net is not there to catch 'The Door' when he falls. For Morrison and his group to resent it is absurd. The theatre that is The Doors – that is basic to their drawing power . . . the audience will grumble, say 'no more', and next time around go to the pop sideshow again, hoping the net will be down and Morrison will take the plunge, and for once they won't get taken. That's showbiz." *(1969)*

John "It's kinda funny to play two of the best sets we've ever done, and then read the reviews knocking the show." *(1969)*

Jim "I was less theatrical, less artificial when I began . . . but now, the audiences we play for are much larger, the rooms much bigger. It's necessary to project more, to exaggerate, almost to the point of grotesqueness. I think that you're a small dot at the end of a large arena, you have to make up for that lack of intimacy with expanded movements." *(1969)*

Ray "Morrison was the road man, the leader who would take you on the trip whilst the rest of us supplied the required energy – this hypnotic, sensual, rhythmic thing, like a snake coiling round your body, and Morrison would work your mind. After The Doors became successful, and Jim fell off the stage – he did do that, he was so gone one time, twirling round like a whirling dervish – the media caught up on that. And when the audience come for that, how are you going to hypnotise them? They want their eyeballs excited. They came to WATCH, they didn't come to listen. At a Doors concert, you were supposed to close your eyes and feel Jim taking you on the trip, the rest of The Doors taking you somewhere you've never been before . . . and at one point, Jim finally said, 'Phooey on you.' That was Miami.'' *(1980)*

Jim ''Being onstage, being one of the central figures, I can only see it from my own viewpoint, but then I suddenly saw things as they really are, that I am, to a degree, just a puppet, controlled by a lot of forces I understand only vaguely.'' *(1969)*

Jim ''I always try to get them to stand up, to feel free to move around anywhere they want to. I like people to be free, not chained.'' *(1969)*

Robbie ''It always bothered me to have police hanging around the shows, waiting to bust us on any word or thing we did, but we expected it – it was all part of the trip.'' *(1978)*

Ray ''They wanted to bust Morrison, Morrison and The Doors. They did in Miami, well, by God, we'll bust 'em in Cincinnati, St. Louis, Chicago, Minneapolis, name your major city.'' *(1980)*

Jim ''I don't think our particular musical style holds up very well in a huge outdoor event. I think that the particular kind of magic that we can breed – when we do – works best in a small theatre.'' *(1969)*

Cashbox ''The Doors, fully cleansed from the unfortunate after effects of their highly publicised Miami exhibition, emerged from many months of self-imposed exile to give a native Los Angeles crowd one of the best and most powerful exhibitions of music performance ever witnessed locally. The Elektra group, who did two 90-minute sets, recorded their efforts for the group's next LP. In totality, The Doors (or for that matter, no group) has ever been so tight, yet so loose. From an instrumental context, Robbie Krieger, Ray Manzarek and John Densmore combined to emit some of the freest-flowing yet melodically-intact instrumental bridges they've ever attempted. And their backing to Jim Morrison was equally effective and, in the process, musically economical.

''But Jim Morrison was the big story. The lines of people didn't form around the circumference of the theatre to dig the instrumentation (though after the performance, many were converted). They came to see the man who was criminally charged with that 'immoral act': could he indeed,

stage a comeback? Morrison came back – and then some. His new visual appearance, and new ease-of-stage presence (as opposed to his previous routine of mock falls and faints) combined to create a new image . . . sort of a thinking-man's-singer', Morrison can no longer be stereotyped simply a 'rock singer'.

''Following a short speech, Morrison and the group burst into gutsy versions of 'Back Door Man' and 'Break On Through', illustrating both Morrison's clear vocal phrasing, and The Doors flair (and apparent ease) for improvisation, lyrically and instrumentally. Then Morrison, on the verge of swallowing the microphone, went through his personal brand of vocal dramatics on familiar Doors tunes, like 'Light My Fire' and 'When The Music's Over'. Of the ample new material The Doors displayed, it ran a gamut from hard rock to uptempo blues and ballads, all led by the new, more confident Jim Morrison. They ended the set, on encore, with a rare performance of their chilling (literally) theatrical piece, 'The Celebration Of The Lizard', which combined poetry and song in a truly sardonic (but artistically successful) mixture.'' *(1969)*

55

Jim "For me, it was never really an act, those so-called performances. It was a life-and-death thing; an attempt to communicate, to involve many people in a private world of thought. I no longer feel I can best do this music through concerts. The belief isn't there." *(1969)*

Ray " The audience has changed; it was no longer the mystical, spiritual union between musicians and audience. That wasn't happening any more." *(1980)*

Ray "All of us have the freedom to explore and improvise within a frame-work. Jim is an improviser with words." *(1978)*

Judith Sims/Los Angeles Free Press

"Lights up, Jim Morrison centre stage unleashed a hoarse scream and followed with a new song, 'Roadhouse Blues', a loping song, almost good-timey. He stood there and sang it, no leaping or prancing. His left hand over his ear, right hand grasping the microphone – the Morrison stance. No leather, no beard, medium hair. For nearly two hours, The Doors played MUSIC. When the instrumental breaks came, Morrison turned his back to us, bending close to the drums, shaking maracas. He didn't even ask the audience for a cigarette. He sang, very well, despite a voice all cracked and husky from four sets in San Francisco. They ran through some songs on the new album and, with only once exception, they recapture that rhythmic lilt of their first album, and the performance has come full circle too. Low key, straightforward, no-nonsense except an occasional scream and one galloping prance across stage, which was too controlled to be irrational. They closed with 'Light My Fire', but they didn't really: they came back and announced they would stay all night if we wanted. We wanted. Several tunes later, Morrison announced a song 'that traditionally finalizes things,' and the opening notes of 'The End' started up. A more relaxed Doors concert I've never seen." *(1970)*

John "It was great, and it was terrible . . . one night great, the next awful – the worst. We played 'Riders On The Storm' for the first time, and the audience loved it. The next night, Jim was as drunk as hell, telling bad jokes on stage. It was horrible. Pathetic." *(1977)*

Ray "Anyone who was there in New Orleans that night saw it. Jim just lost all his energy halfway into the set. You could almost see it leave him; he hung onto the mike stand and his spirit just . . . slipped away. He was finally drained, I guess." *(1978)*

Ray "We were insecure about it. We'd never done singing before. The first time we appeared in public, we were nervous, but after the first couple of numbers, we really got into it." *(1972)*

Robert Weinstein/New York Herald

"Do you remember The Doors? With the death of Jim Morrison, the group faded into obscurity. Following a year of transition, Ray, Robbie and John decided to keep that unique 'Doors sound' alive, and return as a trio. At a recent Carnegie Hall concert, they brought the house down, with screams, shouts and heated outbursts of adulation. Originally, Jim Morrison had provided the centrifugal force for The Doors. A sensuous superstar aura followed him; bold and outlandish, Morrison will go down as a counter-culture hero. He was the musical impetus and few realised the group's strength, musicianship and untapped talent.

"Fortunately, they remained together; the name is the same but musically, they're stronger and more potent. With Ray doing most of the singing, the tone is richer, sharper, more polished. Previously, these three musicians were just part of a band; now the individual virtuosity of each is able to surface. Few realised that Robbie wrote such classics as 'Light My Fire' and 'Touch Me' . . . Confident, singing with a crystal-clear voice, Ray develops his songs slowly, spinning a rock recitative, missing only Morrison's flamboyant gesticulations that motioned an audience to the brink of hysteria. The sound is still hard, pulsating, with long west-coast progressions and acoustic psych-out. By all accounts, the group seems freer and more creative. They can move in any direction, and their new album more than adequately proves it." *(1971)*

Jim "Kids are the future. Kids you can change and mould and influence. That's what's important about a young audience – they're like clean paper waiting to be written on . . . and I'm the ink." *(1969)*

Miami

Jim "There are no rules at a rock concert. Anything is possible." *(1969)*

Larry Mahoney/Miami Herald "It was the night of the riot that did not happen. The Doors, a theatrical rock group, and singer Jim Morrison, pulled out all the stops in an abortive effort to provoke chaos among a huge crowd of Miami young people packed into the Dinner Key Auditorium at $6 a head. The hypnotically erotic Morrison, flouting the laws of obscenity, indecent exposure and incitement to riot, could only stir a minor mob scene towards the end of his Saturday night performance.

"Many of the nearly 12,000 youths said they found the bearded singer's exhibition disgusting. Included in the audience were hundreds of unescorted junior and senior high girls. The Dinner Key exhibition lasted one hour and five minutes. For this, The Doors were paid $25,000. Morrison sang only one song, and that was off-key. For the remainder, he grunted and groaned, gyrated and gestured, in a manner that made Elvis Presley's style seem more staid than a Presbyterian preacher's. His words were inflammatory in a tightly packed crowd . . . It was not meant to be pretty.

"Morrison appeared to masturbate in full view of his audience, screamed obscenities and exposed himself. He also got violent, slugged several officials and threw one of them off the stage before he himself was hurled into the crowd. Morrison, as he does in most of his shows, stole the hat of one of the policemen. The officer wandered about on the stage during the climax of the show trying to get it back. At no time was any effort made by the police to arrest Morrison, even when the mob scene on the bandstand got out of hand. Nor was a report made to headquarters on what had happened. Morrison, who left Miami on Sunday, may yet be arrested for the exhibition, Acting Police Chief Paul M Denham said." *(1969)*

Jim "At Miami, I tried to reduce the myth to absurdity, thereby wiping it out. It just got too much for me to stomach, so I put an end to it one glorious night. I told the audience that they were a bunch of idiots to be members of a crowd, and what were they doing there anyway? Not to listen to some songs by a bunch of good musicians, but for something else . . . so why not admit it and do something about it?" *(1969)*

Robbie "All I remember was, it was a real hot night in Miami. We played at this place called the Dinner Key Auditorium, which was used, I think, more for political meetings and stuff, rather than rock concerts. There was no air conditioning or anything, so by the time we went on stage, the place was a madhouse already – the kids were drunk, or on angel dust, something like that. The place was crazed. Before we went on stage, we were upstairs in the dressing room, and there were a number of policemen up there, and we were joking with them and everything, having a good time.

"So, we finally went down and started to play, and Jim was in one of his more evil moods that night, I would have to say. He'd just had a fight with his girlfriend that day, which didn't exactly help matters . . . and what happened was, there was a lot of confusion on stage. We didn't play one of our best sets, I have to admit. I remember starting one of the songs about three times before we finally got into it – but the kids were having a great time, and the cops were having a great time. They were laughing and boogieing around. And the allegation is that Jim whipped it out, in front of the audience, right? Well I personally never saw that happen, nor did Ray or John, and out of the two or three hundred photographs that were taken that night, there's not one shot that shows that happening.

"There was a lot of movement on stage, jumping around, and finally Jim jumped into the audience. People were just milling around – it looked like a scene from that movie, 'The Snake Pit', where people were rushing around in endless waves. I don't know what Ray did, but finally John and I scooted off stage at that point, because someone was yelling that it was about to collapse, so we beat it upstairs. I don't know how Jim got out of there, but he finally managed to get back out of the audience, and upstairs. He was pretty high by that point, I must confess, and he grabbed one of the cop's hats and was fooling around with it . . . and the cops were in a good mood, so we finally left.

"We all went off to Jamaica for a while, for a little rest, and when we got back, we found a warrant out for Jim's arrest. We didn't know what it was for, and nobody else did either. Finally we learned what had allegedly happened – and that was what the whole Miami trial was about." *(1978)*

Ray . . . but on the other hand "Jim said to the audience, 'That's enough. You didn't come here to hear music, you didn't come to see a good rock 'n' roll band – you came here for something you've never seen before, something greater and bigger than you've ever experienced. What can I do? How 'bout if I show you my cock? Isn't that what you want?' So he took his shirt off and put it in front of himself, and started dancing around holding his shirt down, covering his groin . . . and then he pulled his shirt away – 'Did ya see it, did ya see it? There it is, look, I did it, I did it'." *(1981)*

Ray "I don't think he ever really did it . . . no-one knows for sure. I was five to eight feet away from Jim onstage, and I always have a tendency to put my head down. I'm not concerned with what Jim is doing physically onstage. We didn't have to look at each other – we weren't communicating on that plane . . . so same thing in Miami. I wasn't really looking. He said to me the next day, 'Did I do anything wrong?' And he played along; whether he was putting us on or not, we'll never know, because he looked us right in the eyes and said, 'I don't remember a thing. I had a lot of drinks and I don't even remember getting to Miami.' So who knows? He may have been absolutely honest in that he didn't remember anything." *(1980)*

Jim (attributed) "Uh-oh, I think I exposed myself out there." *(1969)*

John "We didn't get any support from the rock 'n' roll community. They seemed glad." *(1972)*

'The Lords' "But most of the press were vultures, descending on the scene for curious America."

Ray "It was a chance for the righteous to punish those whom they considered unrighteous. There was so much indignation, there was no sense in talking to them. 'You are on the side of the wrong,' they stated, and that was that! It was also a chance for them to make plenty of political hay." *(1980)*

Jim "This trial, and its outcome, won't change my style, because I maintain that I didn't do anything wrong . . . It's actually a very fascinating thing to go through, a thing you can observe. If I have to go to jail, I hope the others will go on and create an instrumental sound of their own, one that doesn't depend on lyrics. Lyrics aren't really that essential in music, anyway." *(1969)*

Jim "I don't know what will happen. I'd guess we'll carry on like this for a while then, to get our vitality back, maybe we'll have to get out of the whole business . . . maybe go to an island by ourselves and start creating again. I might put some of it in a song . . . but the trouble is, the outcome wasn't clear-cut enough for that." *(1969)*

Jim "I was just fed up with the image that had been created around me, which I co-operated with, sometimes consciously, mostly unconsciously." *(1969)*

Jim "Let's just say I was testing the bounds of reality. I was curious to see what would happen. That's all it was: curiosity." *(1969)*

Paris & thereafter

Ray "Jim left for Paris right in the middle of mixing 'LA Woman' – I think we maybe had two more tracks to mix – and he said, 'Hey man, everything's going fine here – why don't you guys finish it up? Pam and I are going to Paris, we're just gonna hang out for a while, see what happens.' So we said, 'OK, talk to you later. Go over there and have a good time, relax, take it easy, write some poetry.'

"What Jim wanted to do, in leaving for France, was to immerse himself in an artistic environment, to get away from Los Angeles, to get away from rock 'n' roll, and all the sensationalist press he's had. Jim was hounded by a lot of yellow journalism and, frankly, he was tired of it. He was tired of being The Lizard King. Jim Morrison was a poet, an artist – he didn't want to be the King of Orgasmic Rock, the King of Acid Rock, The Lizard King. He felt all of those titles that people had hung on him were demeaning to what The Doors were trying to do, so in an effort to escape that, and to recharge his artistic batteries, he went to Paris, the city of art.

"He was going to write, maybe look into a few film projects . . . just getting away, taking a rest. Becoming a poet again. And we'd finished our commitment to Elektra. We'd delivered our seven records over a five, six year period, and were free to go to a new record company, continue making records, *not* make records, whatever. So, as The Doors, we decided to take a long hiatus, and there was really no reason for Jim to be there for the mix. He said, 'You guys finish up – I'm goin' to Paris.' We said, 'OK, man, talk to you later . . .' and I haven't heard from him since." *(1981)*

Ray "Poor Jim had taken the brunt of everything. He was the centre of attraction, and he just needed some time off . . . so, meantime, we were working on new songs, and waiting for Jim to either come back, or say, 'I'm never coming back.' The last thing I heard about Jim, he talked to John on the phone and asked how 'LA Woman' was doing. John told him it was doing great, and Jim got very excited, and said that when he got back, he was ready for the next one. There were definitely things to do, he'd been getting some new ideas, working on his poetry and stuff. Everyone was real optimistic, including Jim and Pam, about the future of The Doors, and about the future of Jim Morrison, poet, rock star, novelist, script writer and even film actor. "Everyone felt pretty positive about the whole thing . . . and then, on July 3, 1971, I got a call from Bill Siddons telling me that Jim Morrison is dead. I said I didn't believe it – I'd heard that story too many times before and this was about the sixth or seventh time Jim had died. But he said, 'No, I think this one is for real.' So I told him, 'OK, you're the acting manager, get your ass over to Paris.' And he said that was exactly what he was going to do.

"When he got over there, he found a sealed coffin, Pamela in near-hysterics and a doctor's certificate, saying that Jim Morrison was indeed dead of a heart stoppage. Of course, when anyone dies, their heart stops . . . but what caused his heart to stop was never said – there was no autopsy, and it was a sealed coffin. I found out just recently that Siddons didn't ask to have the casket opened because, when his father had died, it was also a sealed coffin; and he looked at Jim as though he was a superior being, or at least a father figure, so he never had it opened because he had this sense of deja-vu from when his own father died. That's all I know." *(1980)*

John "We were shocked beyond belief." *(1972)*

Ray "If Pamela was any indication, then Jim was dead. She wasn't faking it. This was a woman who was totally broken up. Jim was her total life and she was devastated, so I assume Jim *was* dead from her reaction, and from the fact that the coffin was put into the ground, and that no-one else has ever said otherwise. But . . . who knows?

He was still up for Miami, and they were going to put his ass in jail. They wanted that guy, they wanted to make an example of him, and he was scared. We were all scared. That was weighing heavily on his mind . . ." *(1980)*

John "I saw Pam a few months afterwards, and when I looked into her eyes, I felt pretty much that Jim was dead . . . on the other hand, he's just about the only person I've met who was wild enough to pull a fast one like that." *(1972)*

Ray "The important thing was always the music, and there were so many things fighting against it that we decided to lay low, quit for a while. Jim was fed-up with everything, and just wanted to go away and write, so by the time he went to Paris, effectively, The Doors were not talking in group terms any more. We were all kinda tired of being Doors." *(1980)*

Robbie "It was all very up in the air as to what we were going to do. We were going to change the name; we'd thought about that, but no-one could come up with anything that didn't sound real pretentious." *(1971)*

Ray "We even thought of calling ourselves 'And The Doors', because at the beginning, it was 'The Doors', and then after a few years it became 'Jim Morrison And The Doors' . . . but we kept 'The Doors' because that's who we still are. There were four of us – now there are three." *(1971)*

John "We sat around, then we jammed a bit, and finally we decided to keep the music going." *(1972)*

Ray "We decided to keep on boogieing. There was no sense in letting it fold up and fall apart. We had too many ideas, so we decided to do them ourselves . . . but it was a tough decision." *(1971)*

Ray "We've spent enough time exploring our subconscious. We've done that along with everybody else in the country. The dark night of the soul is over. We've all been down there in the darkness with the heebie-jeebies for the last few years, and now we finally see the light." *(1972)*

John "We came over to London to find a vocalist and, as we started jamming, we realised more than ever, that when you have a good professional singer, who can do with his voice what someone else can do with their instrument, how much more fluid everything is . . . but that led to writing problems. Everyone, myself included, was writing songs, and all of Ray's were real personal, so it finally got to the point where it was obvious that he was the only one who could sing them, because they're very philosophical, cosmic, whatever, so how could another singer relate to material that was so personal? So, when we first came over, we were still together – sort of – but when we realised how very different our musical directions were heading, Ray split back home . . .'' *(1977)*

Ray ''We wanted to recharge our creative batteries, just as Jim did when he went to Paris,

but it really didn't work out. It was time to close The Doors.'' *(1978)*

Ray ''We were in England, looking for a new singer, new bass player, a second guitar player, whatever – something to give some new life and change The Doors . . . but it just got old, it got boring. We'd been together too long. Without Jim, The Doors just were not The Doors anymore. It wasn't the same band . . . So we went to England to see if we could change things, but we really didn't find anybody. A couple of guys we worked with were good, but I thought it was time to put The Doors to bed, so I said to John and Robbie, 'Listen you guys, let's just pass on this and end it.' And we did.'' *(1978)*

what lif...

John " 'LA Woman' was so much fun to do. Jim called from Paris and we talked about how great it was. I think we would have made another album in that direction." *(1972)*

Robbie "Jim wanted to do more blues, so I think that would've been the next step – solid blues. We would have done that for at least one more album, maybe two. After that, who knows? I don't really think I could've seen The Doors existing into the seventies. I think we would have probably given up and gone into movies, or something." *(1978)*

Ray "I think The Doors would have been making music very much like 'An American Prayer'. I think we'd have been doing real poetry and music things. Songs would have still been important, but we'd have probably gone on to poetry, music song, another song, more poetry, a keyboard playing by itself, a guitar playing by itself. It would have fragmented itself from strictly songs to a much more theatrical thing. An album would have been a 45-minute presentation of a body of ideas, a series of pieces . . . very much like 'An American Prayer'. Jim actually recorded that just before he left for Paris, on his birthday, December 8, 1970, and he had the idea to do an extended poem piece of some sort or another, working with sound effects, music, whatever.'' *(1978)*

Ray ''One of the saddest aspects of my life –

other than Jim leaving this planet — is that we never got to play 'LA Woman' live. We were going to take Jerry Scheff with us; we were even thinking of taking a rhythm guitarist with us so that we could go from a four-piece to a six-piece band. I was really looking forward to that, 'because Jerry would have freed me. Let me play organs, synth-esizers, string synth clavinet, all that stuff.'' *(1978)*

Doors on the Doors

7

Robbie "This group is so serious. It's the most serious group that ever was, that ever will be." *(1967)*

Ray "There are things you know about, and things you don't – the known and the unknown – and in between are the doors. That's us. We're saying that you're not only spirit, you're also this very sensuous being, and that's not evil. It's a really beautiful thing. Hell seems so much more fascinating and bizarre than heaven. You have to 'break on through to the other side' to become the whole being." *(1967)*

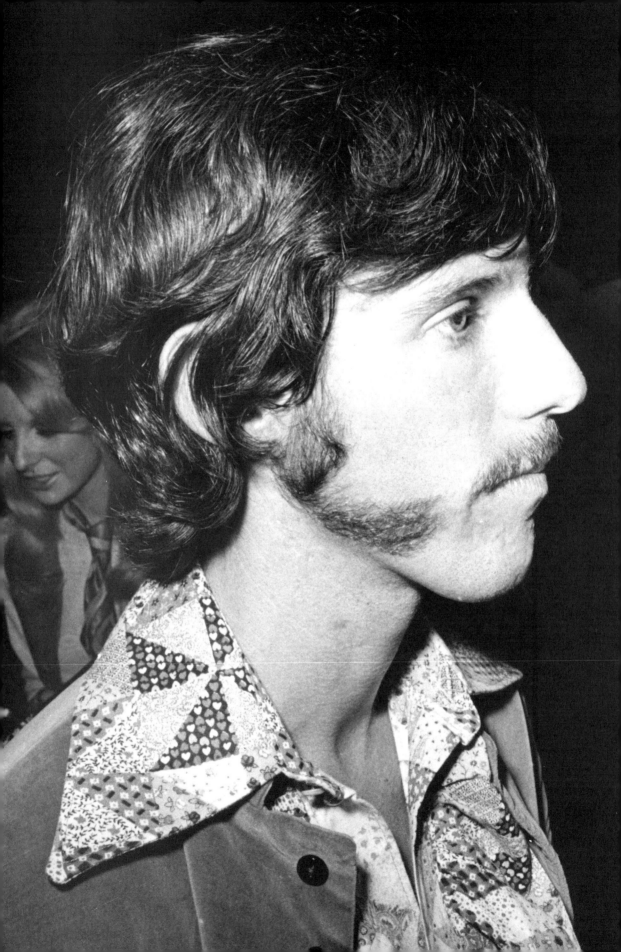

Jim "We're a partnership, artistically and financially. We share equally. In the beginning, a lot of it was to keep the unit together. We have a very different vision of reality, different points to make." *(1969)*

Jim "As a guitar player, Robbie's more complex, and my thing is more in a blues vein; long, rambling, basic and primitive. It's just the difference between any two poets is very great." *(1969)*

John "I can see that someone who isn't familiar with our music would want to say, 'Now what does this damned 'blue bus' thing mean?' You tell them, if the guys in the band don't even know what it means, they don't have to worry about it. I never tried to think what the hell it all means. It's just there, it's just one of Jim's poems. I'm not saying that we're all super-literate – although we are, Jim's read all the goddam poetry there is to read, but that's not what I'm saying: I'm just saying that we do it, it comes out that way and people dig it, so it's justified. If you do something that everyone likes, why bother analysing it? Everyone's moved, so OK." *(1968)*

Jim "Los Angeles is a city looking for a ritual to join its fragments, and The Doors are looking for such a ritual also. A kind of electric wedding. We hide ourselves in the music to reveal ourselves." *(1969)*

Ray "We all play a lead and subjugation thing with each other. When Jim gets into something, I'm able to give of that area within myself. We may look cool, but we are really evil, insidious cats behind Jim. We instigate the violence in him. A lot of the time, he doesn't feel particularly angry, but the music just drives him to it." *(1970)*

Jim "I can just look at Ray and know when I've gone too far." *(1969)*

Jim "We are from the West. The world we suggest should be of a new wild West, a sensuous, evil world, strange and haunting. The path of the sun . . ." *(1967)*

Ray "Our music has to do with operating in the dark areas within yourself. A lot of people are operating on the love trip, and that's nice, but there are two sides to this thing. There's a black, evil side as well as a white, love side, and what we're trying to do is to come to grips with that and realise it. Sensual is probably the word that best fits it." *(1968)*

Jim "Think of us as erotic politicians." *(1967)*

John "You have to search and enquire if you want to find something out, or you have to open a Door." *(1968)*

Jim "The Doors are basically a blues-orientated band with heavy doses of rock 'n' roll, a modicum of jazz, some popular elements and a minute quantity of classical influences . . . but, basically, a white blues band." *(1970)*

Ray "Here in Los Angeles, the young people especially are very excited, very alive. The space age is here right now: this is the city of the future, of the 21st century. The rest of the world's going to look like LA in a couple of hundred years time." *(1968)*

Ray "The Doors have always had history on their minds, so we saw to it that every record we made, we tried to make it up to the top level of our standards. Nothing was put out just for the sake of making a buck. Even when we played the Whiskey, we really believed we were going to take over the country, turn it around, make the perfect society." *(1980)*

Robbie "Most groups today aren't true groups. In a true group, all the members create the arrangements amongst themselves. Here, we use everyone's ideas." *(1980)*

Jim "I think The Doors were very timely, the music and the ideas were very timely. They may seem naive now, but back then, people were into some very weird things. You could say things like we did, and almost half-ass believe them. A combination of good musicianship and timelessness. We weren't trend conscious or anything like that. We were doing exactly what we would have been doing anyway. It came at the right time, and we could get away with expressing sentiments like that." *(1970)*

Robbie "I think a lot of success can endanger your artistic side. Once you get big like that, you have to be touring all the time, and all the pressures make it hard to create . . . but as long as you're capable of creating stuff that will bring joy or happiness to people, then you're obligated to do it." *(1978)*

Robbie "With Jim, it was like the band, and the Voice of God up front, and everybody seemed to be overshadowed by that voice." *(1980)*

Robbie "I hope we made a lot of people happy." *(1972)*

Jim "We started with music, then went into theatre, but it was so shitty that we went back into music, back to where we started, just being a rock band. And the music has gotten progressively better, tighter, more interesting and professional, but I think people resent that. I think they resent the fact that, when things didn't change overnight in that great renaissance of spirit, emotion and revolutionary sentiment, that we're still here doing good music." *(1970)*

Jim "I think we're the band you love to hate — it's been that way from the beginning. We're universally despised, and I kinda relish the whole situation. Why, I don't know: I think that we're on a monstrous ego-trip, and people resent it . . . they hate us because we're so good!" *(1970)*

Ray "We've all shattered ourselves a long time ago. That was what early rock was all about — an attempt to shatter 2,000 years of culture. Now we're working on what happens after you've been shattered." *(1967)*

sex & drugs & rock & roll & booze & politics & films & stuff

Robbie "There were two forces working, one of change and the other that wanted things to stay the same and not be too far-out . . . and there's always the balance that has to be there." *(1968)*

Jim "When you make your peace with authority, you become an authority." *(1969)*

Ray "We wanted to change the world, make the world a better place to live in, and we were trying to do it. The fact that it wasn't happening – OK, a temporary setback, it was still going to happen." *(1980)*

John "I felt that we were the ones who stopped the goddam war . . . a reflection of what everyone was trying to say. We were trying to express what was going on: Wake up, listen!" *(1977)*

Jim "To me, politics is nothing more than the search of certain individuals for private power. They can cloak it in any idealogical, romantic or philosophical terms they want, but it's essentially a private search for power." *(1969)*

'The Lords' "Chance is a survival of religion in the modern city as is theatre, more often cinema, the religion of possession."

Jim "Your politics, or your religion, is what you devote the majority of your time to. It might be a woman. It might be a drug. It might be money or alcohol . . . might be literature." *(1969)*

Jim "I haven't studied politics that much, really. It just seems to me that you have to be in a state of constant revolution, or you're dead. There always has to be a revolution. It has to be a constant thing, not something that's going to change things, and that's it, the revolution's going to solve everything. It has to be every day." *(1970)*

Jim "I don't think so far that politics has been a major theme in my songs. It's there in a few, but it's a very minor theme. Politics is people and their interaction with other people, so you really cannot separate it from anything." *(1970)*

'The New Creatures' "Life goes on absorbing war."

'The New Creatures' "We reap bloody crops on war fields."

'An American Prayer' "Do you know we are being led to slaughters by placid admirals/and that fat slow generals are getting obscene on young blood."

Jim "We like anything which is a violent reaction against the norm." *(1968)*

Jim "Sex is full of lies. The body tries to tell the truth, but it's usually too battered with rules to be heard. We cripple ourselves with lies. Most people have no idea of what they're missing, our society places a supreme value on control, on hiding what you feel. It mocks primitive culture and prides itself on the suppression of natural instincts and impulses." *(1969)*

Jim "Sex can be a liberation, but it can also be an entrapment. Puritanical attitudes die slowly. How can sex be a liberation if you don't really want to touch your body, if you're trying to escape from it?" *(1968)*

John "Acid gave us visions, and the realisation of the power we had." *(1972)*

Jim "Everyone smokes grass, so I guess you don't think of it as a drug any more, but three years ago there was that wave of hallucinogenics. I don't think anyone has the strength to sustain those trips forever, then you go into narcotics, of which one is alcohol. Instead of trying to think more, you kill thought. Painkillers. That's what people have gotten into." *(1969)*

Jim "You can go down to any corner store, and it's right there, across the table. That's why I like alcohol . . . and because it's traditional." *(1969)*

Jim "I went through a period when I drank a lot. I had a lot of pressure hanging over me that I couldn't handle, and I was also drinking as a way to cope with living in a crowded environment, and also as the product of boredom. But I enjoy drinking: it loosens people up and stimulates conversation sometimes. Somehow, it's like gambling: you go out for a night of drinking, and you don't know where you'll end up the next morning. It could be good, could be a disaster. It's a throw of the dice." *(1969)*

Jim "I can gauge everything so's I can stay in one place: every sip is another chance at bliss." *(1968)*

Ray "America hasn't produced anybody heavy in rock 'n' roll as far as I'm concerned. Maybe Bob Dylan – he did some good stuff, real good stuff, no doubt about that. He's since become a little weird, as far as I'm concerned." *(1968)*

Jim "Some brilliant kid will come along and be popular. I can see a lone artist with a lot of tapes and, like, an extension of the Moog synthesizer – a keyboard with the complexity and richness of a full orchestra. We'll hear about that in a couple of years." *(1969)*

Jim "Rock 'n' roll . . . it was after the Korean War was ended, and there was a psychic purge. There seemed to be a need for an underground explosion, an eruption, so maybe after the Vietnam War is over, there will again be a need for a life force to express and assert itself." *(1969)*

Jim "The initial flash is over. This thing they used to call rock 'n' roll, it got decadent. The energy is gone. There is no longer a belief. The English sparked a revival, it went very far, it was articulate – and then it became self-conscious, which I think is the death of any movement." *(1969)*

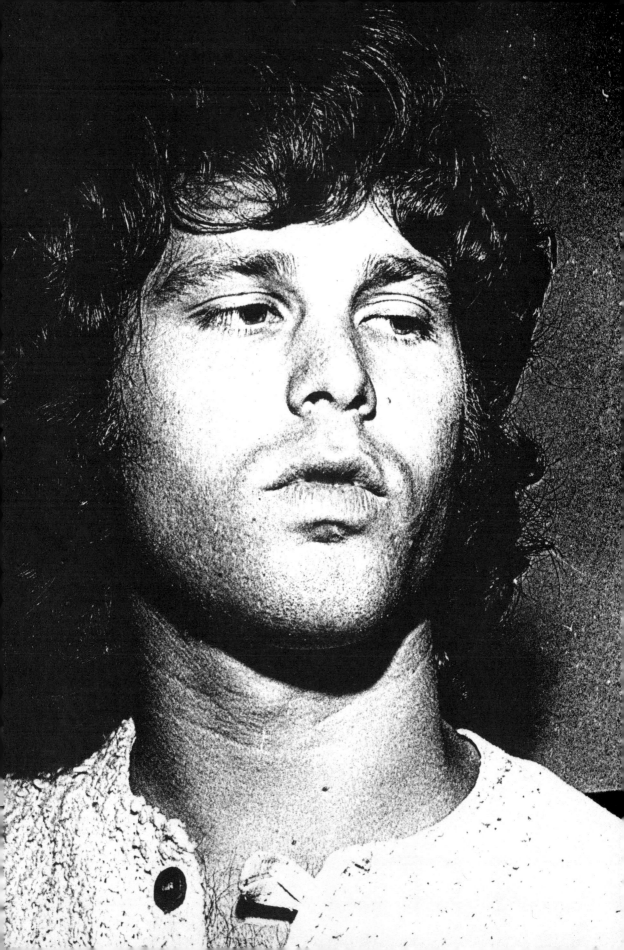

Jim "Sometimes . . . I like to think of the history of rock 'n' roll like the origin of Greek drama. That started out on the threshing floors during the crucial seasons, and was originally a band of acolytes dancing and singing. Then, one day, a possessed person jumped out of the crowd and started imitating a god . . ." *(1968)*

Jim "Rock 'n' roll is a perfect mix of white music and black music, and that's why I love it." *(1969)*

Ray "The total statement of rock 'n' roll and its

audience is revolutionary. Long hair, for example, is an obvious up-front revolutionary statement.'' *(1980)*

Jim ''This whole thing started with rock 'n' roll, and now it's out of control.'' *(1968)*

Jim ''More and more, I think that the three-minute single is pointless.'' *(1969)*

Jim ''Rock is going to become a dumb fad very soon. Jazz is coming back into it . . . but for me, it has to be theatre. I don't care if the critics don't like it – that's not what counted when we started, and it's not what counts now we've made it.'' *(1969)*

Jim ''I'm interested in film because, to me, it's the closest approximation in art that we have to the actual flow of consciousness.'' *(1969)*

Ray ''At school, at UCLA, I was always interested in film, as it seemed to combine my interests in drama, visual arts, music – and the profit motive!'' *(1972)*

'The Lords' '' Films are collections of dead pictures which are given artificial insemination. Film spectators are quiet vampires.'' *(1969)*

Jim ''That's what I love about films – they're so perishable. One big nuclear explosion, and all the celluloid melts . . . and that's why poetry appeals to me so much, because it's so eternal. As long as there are people, they'll remember words and combinations of words. Nothing else can survive a holocaust except poetry and songs. No-one can remember an entire novel. No-one can describe a film, or a painting. But as long as there are humans, poetry and song continue.'' *(1969)*

Jim ''Whoever controls the media, controls the mind.'' *(1969)*

Jim ''The good thing about film is that there are no experts. Anybody can assimilate the whole history of film by himself, which you can't do in any of the other arts. There are no experts, so in theory, any student knows as much as any professor.'' *(1969)*

Jim ''Film compresses everything. It packs a lot of energy into a small space.'' *(1969)*

'The Lords' ''We are content with the 'given' in sensation's quest.''

'The Lords' ''More or less, we're all afflicted with the psychology of the voyeur.''

Jim ''The attraction of the cinema lies in the fear of death.'' *(1969)*

Jim ''Film is a hard medium to break into. It's so much more complex than music. You need so many more people and so much equipment. I like the rock medium because of its directness, the direct contact with the audience.'' *(1969)*

Jim ''Is there anything worse than a really bad photograph? You know that it's not you, but someone has chosen to view you in that way.'' *(1969)*

'The Lords' ''Modern life is a journey by car.''

Jim ''America was conceived in violence. All Americans are outlaws. Americans are attached to violence. TV is the invisible shield against bare reality. Twentieth century culture's disease is the inability to feel reality. People cluster to TV, soap operas, movies, rock idols and they have wild emotions over symbols; but in the reality of their own lives, they're emotionally dead.'' *(1969)*

Jim ''Each generation wants new symbols, new people, new names. They want to divorce themselves from their predecessors.'' *(1969)*

'The Lords' ''We are obsessed with heroes who live for us and whom we punish.''

the importance of being Jim

Jim "I think of myself as an intelligent, sensitive human with the soul of a clown, which always forces me to blow it at the most important moments." *(1969)*

Ray "He lived very intensely. He squeezed a lot of years into his 27." *(1980)*

Robbie "He was always the same. Crazy. Actually, he was much more wild and crazy when he wasn't onstage. He was always mad that he didn't become bigger faster, like The Beatles or something. That was his only complaint." *(1980)*

John "There was nothing he wouldn't take or try to make himself madder. Jim was bent on self-destruction, I guess. I don't know how much longer we could've held together." *(1980)*

Jim "I think the highest and the lowest points are the important ones. Anything else is just . . . in between. I want the freedom to try everything." *(1968)*

Ray "Jim is unpredictable. On tour, he may not spend as much as 10 minutes in the hotel, for example. He may disappear, and even we won't see him except for the shows. We've learned not to get uptight about it. It's just the way he is. You never can tell." *(1968)*

in their own words **the doors**

'The Lords' "The Stranger was sensed as the greatest menace in ancient communities."

Jim "I'm not a new Elvis . . . I just think I'm lucky. I've found a perfect medium to express myself in. Music, writing, theatre, action – I'm doing all those things. I like to write, but songs are special; I find music liberates my imagination. When I sing my songs in public, that's a dramatic act – not just acting as in a theatre but social acting, real acting." *(1969)*

Jim "I'm the square of the western hemisphere. Whenever somebody'd say something groovy, it'd blow my mind. Now, I'm learning. I hate people. I don't need them. If I had an axe I'd kill everyone . . . except my friends." *(1968)*

'The Lords/Notes On Vision' "All games contain the idea of death."

Ray "Jim Morrison as Dionysius, a Greek god reincarnate. Whereas Apollo was the god of light, clear thought, logical thinking, Dionysius was the god of feeling, spontaneity, the dance, music. Dionysius enters the body through the ears, via music, through primitive rhythms, and Jim was Dionysius personified. The man onstage was an absolute genius, a human theatricon. From one performance to the next, you never knew what he was going to be. Sometimes a devil, sometimes a saint. Sometimes an angel, sometimes a demon from hell, the Banshee himself.
"I've never seen a performer like Jim – it was as if it wasn't Jim performing, but a shaman. Traditionally, a shaman was the man of a tribe who would go on a voyage in his mind, who would let his astral body project out into space and, in a sense, heal the tribe, find things that were needed for the safety and well-being of the tribe, for the continuance of the species. So, in a modern sense, Jim was exactly the same thing. He always said, 'We may never do this again, so let's do it for real, right here and now on this stage, because if we don't we may never have the opportunity again. The future is uncertain and the end is always near, and if we don't do it now, if we don't commune with the gods, with our own feelings, our own spirituality, then we've lost this golden opportunity, this moment in reality that may never come again'.

"Jim was always very aware of the fact that each moment was precious, a jewel, a drop of time, and that it was all we had. We had the present. Not the past. Not the future. When The Doors stepped out on a stage, all there was was the present. This holy moment: four guys on stage, an audience out there and the energy flowing back and forth between them in what became, in a sense, a communion. My energy had been totally spent, and I felt cleansed of any evil and darkness. We walked out of a concert feeling absolutely in touch with the universe, and *that*, if any, was the message of Jim Morrison – 'Get in touch with yourself. When you do that, you'll be in touch with the Gods, you *become* Gods.' Jim's message was that every man is a *God* – all you have to do is realise it." *(1978)*

Robbie "Be careful. He'll do what you say, and do what you say, and do what you say . . . but then one day he'll do something very strange and violent." *(1968)*

Jim "I think that more than writing and music, my greatest talent is that I have an instinctive knack of self-image propagation. I was very good at manipulating publicity with a few little phrases like 'erotic politicians'. Having grown up with TV and mass magazines, I knew instinctively what people would catch on to, so I dropped those little jewels here and there, seemingly very innocently; of course, I was just calling signals." *(1969)*

Jim "I always liked the things I read. Of course – they were about me. But they were concentrating on my progenitive organ too much, and weren't paying attention to the fact that I was a fairly healthy young male, who also had something more than the standard arms, legs, ribs, eyes and so on – had a cerebellum, the full equipment. The press always does that." *(1970)*

Robbie "He didn't mind people bugging him about being a star, because that's what he was trying to be . . . but he did find it hard to live up to some of the legends, especially with the girls; they expected him to have a four-foot cock, or something like that." *(1980)*

Ray "It was always difficult working with Jim.

The man was a genius, and genius is allowed a very schizophrenic behaviour. Sometimes he could be an angel, sometimes a devil . . . but that's what was inside of him, that's what was brilliant about the man. You never knew from day to day which Jim Morrison was going to show up; but whichever one it was, the words were going to be brilliant. It was hard to work with him, but on the other hand, it was a great joy to work with a man who's such a genius." *(1980)*

Jim "I like singing blues – those free, long blues trips where there's no specific beginning or end. It just gets into a groove, and I can keep making things up. Singing has all the things I like. It's involved with writing and with music. There's a lot of acting, and it has this other thing, a physical element, a sense of the immediate. When I sing, I create characters. Hundreds of them." *(1969)*

Jim "People seek tyrants. They worship and support them. They co-operate with restrictions and rules, and they become enchanted with the violence involved in their brief, token rebellion. The LA cops are idealists, almost fanatical in believing the rightness of their cause. They have a whole philosophy behind their tyranny." *(1969)*

Robbie "I've never seen anybody else from our generation who could put words together like Jim could. He wrote some of his best stuff towards the end. If he'd been more disciplined, he could have done even greater things, but there was nothing you could do about it. People would tell Jim to drink less, and he would just take them out and get them drunk." *(1980)*

John "It's really difficult when you start out . . . you'll do anything. Then you get a little flush, and I guess that's why Jim eventually grew his beard and put some weight on. He wasn't trying to reject it, just move away from it, from the Mick Jagger image. He wanted to be a poet and a writer." *(1980)*

Jim "I'll always be a word man, better than a bird man."

Jim "I am The Lizard King, I can do anything."

Jim "I've always liked reptiles. I used to see the universe as a mammoth snake, and I used to see all the people and objects, landscapes, as little pictures in the facets of their scales. I think peristaltic motion is the basic life movement. Swallowing, digestion, the rhythms of sexual intercourse. We must not forget that the lizard and the snake are identified with the unconscious, with the forces of evil. There's something deep in the human memory that reacts very strongly to reptiles. Even if you've never seen one, the snake embodies everything we fear." *(1968)*

Jim "It's all done tongue-in-cheek – I don't think too many people realise that. It's not supposed to be taken seriously. It's supposed to be ironic." *(1968)*

Ray "Morrison, he took it all the way, and I think that's the thing America loved about him. I think one of the reasons that people are still intrigued with Jim Morrison is because his themes were universal. Morrison was talking about a lot more than the late days of hippiedom, or the fact that we were recording in 1967/68/69/70 doesn't necessarily limit us to that time-frame, when the revolution was happening, when the riots were happening in England that we've been sort of linked with.

"We've always felt The Doors' themes were, as Jim used to say, primeval, back to basics, feelings of humanity. What we were talking about, and what Jim is saying on 'An American Prayer', is life itself. He's not talking about any transient or trendy sort of thing, he's talking about a man on the planet. Where did we come from? What are we doing here? Where are we going? What happens at the end? That's why Jim was, as some people say, obsessed with death . . . but it wasn't an obsession, it was an understanding that death is our constant companion.

"If there's one thing you know on this planet, it's that you're going to die, and you'd better be able to come to peace with that idea. And, if you can come to terms with that, all of a sudden your life takes on a new meaning, blossoms open because you don't have to worry about, 'My God, I'm going to die – we've got to prevent my death.' You can't do that. You have to live closely with your death, and I think Jim did. It was right over his shoulder, waiting there all the time." *(1980)*

Jim "I wouldn't mind dying in a plane crash. It'd

be a good way to go. I don't want to die in my sleep, or of old age, or OD . . . I want to feel what it's like. I want to taste it, hear it, smell it. Death is only going to happen to you once; I don't want to miss it." *(1969)*

Jim (who also held this view . . .) "I'd hope to die at about 120 with a sense of humour and a nice comfy bed. I wouldn't want anyone around, I'd just want to quietly drift off. But I'm still holding out for science. I think that in our lifetime, it has a chance to conquer death. I think it's very possible." *(1970)*

Jim "Living in LA is no big deal. It's an anonymous city, and I live an anonymous life." *(1969)*

Jim "We're like actors, turned loose in this world to wander in search of a phantom, endlessly searching for a half-formed shadow of our lost reality." *(1968)*

Jim "I've had a good time these past few years. I've met a lot of interesting people and seen things that I probably wouldn't have seen in 20 years of ordinary living. I can't say I regret it but, if I had to do it all over again, I think I'd have gone for the quiet, artist-plodding-away-in-his-own-garden trip . . . or maybe a corporation executive. I kinda like the image. Big office. Secretary." *(1969)*

Jim "I'd hate to think I'd stop having anything to do with music, but I think that in the future, I'll tend towards an exclusive film involvement." *(1969)*

Jim "I'm interested in anything about revolt, disorder, chaos, especially any activity that seems to have no meaning." *(1968)*

John "Jim was a pretty smart fellow. That's why he had so many ups and downs." *(1972)*

Jim "I'm beginning to think it's easier to scare people than to make them laugh." *(1970)*

Jim "I like people who shake other people up and make them feel uncomfortable." *(1969)*

Robbie "Jim was the toughest to please. I wouldn't say he dominated musically, but lyrically he certainly did." *(1977)*

Jim "A friend is someone who lets you have total freedom to be yourself." *(1968)*

Jim "I'd like to start a magazine, newspaper thing in LA sometime. The trouble is, I'll only do it if I could finance it myself, so that I wouldn't need to advertise. You know, like those little one-issue magazines and manifestos the Dadaists and surrealists used to put out." *(1970)*

Jim "Woodstock seemed to me to be just a bunch of young parasites being spoon-fed these three or four days of . . . you know what I mean, they looked like the victims and dupes of a culture, more than anything. Of course, that may be sour grapes because I wasn't there, not even as a spectator, so . . . But I think that, even though they're a mess, and even though they're not what they pretend to be, some free celebration of a young culture, it's still better than nothing, and I'm sure that some of the people take away a kind of myth back to the city with them." *(1970)*

Jim "Play is an open event. It's free. Little kids are like dogs. They run around, touch things, sing a song. Well, actors play like that, and musicians too, and you dig watching someone play, because that's the way people are supposed to be – free, like animals. Animals don't build war machines and invest millions of dollars in attacking other countries whose political ideas don't happen to agree with their own." *(1968)*

Jim "Expose yourself to your deepest fear: after that, fear has no power, and the fear of freedom shrinks and vanishes. You *are* free." *(1969)*